Play Like Pep Guardiola's Barcelona

A Soccer Coach's Guide

Agustín Peraita

BENNION KEARNY

Published by Bennion Kearny Ltd

Copyright © 2016 MC Sports/Marketing Murillo

Original Title: Quiero que mi equipo juegue como el F.C.Barcelona de Guardiola (Preparacion Futbolistica)

This edition published by agreement with MC Sports/Marketing Murillo

ISBN: 978-1-910515-63-1

Published by Bennion Kearny Limited
6 Woodside
Churnet View Road
Oakamoor
ST10 3AE

www.BennionKearny.com

About The Author

Agustin Peraita is FCBareclona Sao Paulo Escola Technical Director. He is a UEFA Pro Coach and has experience as head coach in Catalan Youth teams such as CE Sabadell, UE Vilassar or UDA Gramanet.

The Spanish version of his book "I want my team to play as Guardiola´s FCBarcelona" was published in Spain in July 2015. It is already into its second edition. He is a frequent contributor to Marti Perarnau's (Guardiola's authorized biographer) tactical magazine *The Tactical Room*.

About the Lead Translator

Iñaki Samaniego is one of the most up and coming goalkeeper coaches in Europe. Born in Sevilla, and after living and working for several years in England and Holland, he is now back in Spain where he is involved in several goalkeeping projects. Iñaki has coached at important clubs like RCD Espanyol in Barcelona and ADO Den Haag in The Hague. Besides coaching, Iñaki also gives presentations and practices about goalkeeping, having shared his knowledge about the position in countries like Sweden, Scotland, Holland, England, Poland and of course Spain. Last but not least, Iñaki is also an avid translator, having translated several football-related books like the Bestseller *Soccer Tough*. If you want to know more about him, you can follow him on Twitter on @InakiSamaniego

About this book

This book has been translated from the original Spanish title *Quiero que mi equipo juegue como el F.C.Barcelona de Guardiola*, and therefore uses some terms that would not form the everyday language of football in the English-speaking world. Efforts have been made to remain as faithful to the original text as possible and this can, on occasion, lead to testing sections for the reader. Some content simply does not translate directly nor easily.

As the book progresses and becomes more technical, greater focus is required to truly absorb the gems and inside knowledge concerning Pep Guardiola's Barcelona. Someone once said that by talking quietly, people strain to listen and therefore focus more on every word you say. That is a great analogy for this book. Read it slowly, in smaller bursts, with a pen and paper ready, to truly absorb and appreciate the information.

Foreword

When you watched the 2008-2012 Barcelona team, you kind of felt that they knew a footballing secret that you didn't. You felt that no matter how many games you watched them play, there was information about their preparation, about their training methods, and their convictions, that was top secret and held in a concealed vault somewhere in Cataluña. Coaches from all over the world set out on a pilgrimage to the training ground and Academy there to find and learn this secret. Most left still wondering – but probably insisted (when they got home) that their players take part in rondo exercises before training.

Although I was always an admirer of the Barcelona Way, I truly fell in love with the Barcelona team of Pep Guardiola following their crushing win against Real Madrid in November 2010. The 5-0 scoreline didn't flatter them. That evening, on the stage of *El Classico* no less, they utterly humbled and humiliated one of the greatest teams on the planet. The way they moved the ball made an opposition full of superstars, and one of the game's best coaches, look distinctly average. This was the game and the moment when I knew I had to learn more. I knew I had to figure out their 'secrets' to understand – from a coaching perspective – how this team worked, and how this coach operated. I have re-watched that game over and over again and still pick up something new every time.

When you sat down to watch Barcelona, you never felt that they were going to do anything that surprised you. Yes, they would mesmerize you with their style of play, but I rarely remember them making wholesale changes to their approach. They were, in many ways, quite predictable. They would play out from the back using short passes, whether the opposition pressed them high or dropped off to defend their own penalty area. They would aim to completely out-pass you and do so with long successions of short passes. They would press you high and early in an attempt to win the ball back close to your goal. They would play an extremely open 4-3-3 (although Guardiola pushed the boundaries formation-wise late in his Barça tenure). Wingers would stay wide until late in attacks, they would use a single holding midfielder, and both full-backs would join in offensively with no invitation. All teams knew this was coming, yet very few could actually do anything about it. Predictable maybe, but most impressively, they remained virtually unstoppable.

With their predictability were changes and surprises that were more subtle, yet often more jaw-dropping. The 5'9" Javier Mascherano became a central defender. Not only that, but so did Yaya Touré – in a Champions League Final no less. This is the same Yaya Touré whose subsequent defensive performances as a midfield player continue to see him heavily criticized at Manchester City. Barça would dominate the ball so much that the more midfielders the team had, the better. Further changes saw Lionel Messi, a lightweight winger, became the main striker, or at least the false 9 version of one – which Guardiola astonishingly test-drove during a must-win league game at the Santiago

Bernabéu, home of their great rivals, Real Madrid!

The story of small, lightweight players forms the backdrop to one of modern football's great stories. It is certainly a story of Guardiola's team and his greatest achievements. Not only did Barcelona dominate Spain and Europe through high level technical and tactical play, but they changed the landscape of how football was perceived. They did not just win trophies and accolades, this team and this coach changed modern football.

Even in removed footballing cultures like England's – where height, mass, and physicality are prized heavily – coaches began to look at Barcelona and wonder whether there was another way. Barcelona was not a flash in the pan. They were consistent champions. Even their goalkeeper Víctor Valdés and 'hardman' centre-back Carles Puyol were both under 6 feet tall. Diminutive midfielders Xavi Hernández and Andreas Iniesta suddenly blossomed and became the go-to names for any player, coach, or pundit who dared to suggest that physical stature was a prerequisite for professional footballers. Young players all over the world were told by Pep and Barcelona that their size didn't matter after all – they just needed to find a place that accepted them. And what's more is these players were the team's spine – goalkeeper, centre-back, midfield, and then of course, 'striker' Messi. For every Abidal, they had a Dani Alves; for every 6 foot plus Pique and Busquets, they had a Villa and Pedro. If a team playing on the greatest football stage of all could 'trust' the little guys, why shouldn't an Academy youth team or an amateur local club?

Two of the aforementioned players would also become measures for Guardiola's methods around the promotion of youth. One of Pep's early considerations at the Camp Nou was to rid the team of its flamboyant but increasingly ineffective and troublesome superstars. Although Samuel Eto'o earned a reprieve, Ronaldinho and Deco were shown the door in no-nonsense fashion. As they exited, two unheard-ofs stood waiting to enter.

In Guardiola's fist summer as Barcelona Head Coach, both Pedro Rodríguez and Sergio Busquets were promoted from Barça B, and, in no time, became key players for their club, and also for the Spanish national team who exported Guardiola's work onto the international scene. Seven of Spain's starting line-up in the 2010 World Cup Final were Barcelona players – six of them were from their youth academy at La Masia (Cesc Fabregas was to come on as a substitute that night – and provide the World Cup winning assist for Iniesta). A frightening statistic at any level of the game.

Since leaving Barcelona, Pep Guardiola has continued to consistently push the boundaries both technically and tactically with his teams – but he has also adapted hugely to his new environments. There is little doubt that 'his' Bayern Munich team bore the hallmarks of what you would now consider the Guardiola blueprint – dominating possession, quick intricate play, high pressing, etc. However, they could seamlessly transition from one formation to another – it was best at some points to not even try to work out what formation he was using. As Guardiola himself said, formations are phone numbers, it the actions of the players and the coverage of spaces on the pitch that matters. His defensive focus became about preventing counter-attacks, something he mentioned over and over again in Bundesliga pre-match press conferences. You would happily see goalkeeper Manuel Neuer standing in the centre-circle while his team attacked to allow this tactic to thrive – something Neuer has been seen doing for Germany since. Pep was altering his way to meet German needs, but his blueprint remained.

If Guardiola's blueprint was obvious when his native Spain won the World Cup, it was also obvious when his adopted home, Germany, won the competition in 2014. While Germany had a root and branch overhaul of its playing structures after 2000 and independent of Guardiola, having the country's biggest and best club playing high pressure, possession-based, free-flowing football would provide the German national team with World Cup winning benefits. It truly is a unique achievement to lead the most dominant team in the country – and produce the spine and the style that the national team would use to win a World Cup – not just once, but twice!

And on to Manchester City he goes and we all wait with bated breath to see the long-term effects he can have on them, and also on the wider Premier League – and maybe even the soul of the English game. His competition is stiff, where old foes Mourinho and Klopp lie in wait, as well as potential new adversaries such as Conte and Wenger – and indeed the more traditional Pulis and Moyes, and maybe the closest thing England has to Pep – Eddie Howe.

To trace the evolution of Guardiola, and the way of his teams, we must go back to the beginnings at Barcelona. Above all else, this tenure changed me as a coach. It changed me tremendously. It taught me to stick to my principles. It taught me to explore the game and to push the technical and tactical boundaries of myself and the players. It taught me to truly value the little guy. It taught me you could play without both centre-backs and strikers and make it work. He continues to teach me from afar. The contents of this book will teach you much more. Enjoy.

Ray Power | @power_ray

Ray Power is a former Academy Coach, Academy Manager, and FA Coach Educator. He is now the Technical Director in Tanzania, working alongside Sunderland AFC, and the Tanzanian Football Federation as coach educator and Elite Football Academy manager. Ray also leads extensive talent identification projects in the country. Ray is the author of the acclaimed football coaching books *Making The Ball Roll: A Complete Guide to Youth Football for the Aspiring Soccer Coach, Soccer Tactics 2014: What The World Cup Taught Us*, and The *Deliberate Soccer Practice* books.

Table of Contents

Introduction

Once every decade or so, a team emerges that amazes the world. And, once a generation, a team emerges that creates a new *era* in football. The new era leads to revolutionary tactics and ideas that break with the 'status quo' of the game and which drive new schools of thought, analysis, and training.

One of these legendary teams, and one of these playing revolutions, was implemented by Futbol Club Barcelona during the 2009-2010 season. A team managed by Josep "Pep" Guardiola Sala.

Pep Guardiola and his team amazed the world with an unprecedented style of football. At the time, only a few could see beyond the technical excellence, the taste for overwhelming ball possession, and the high pace of play (dubbed 'tiki-taka'[1] by the press). Over time, a few authors started highlighting the key tactics of Pep's model, but a deep and thorough analysis of each part of his model did not spread through the football community. As a consequence, most coaches, journalists, players and managers have taken the visible 'superficial' factors from the tactical offerings of Guardiola and misinterpreted the true identity of this model of play.

"The Barça of Guardiola has done a lot of harm to football"

This is a phrase heard on many occasions, over the last few years, on football pitches of all levels, from Under-12 to the highest leagues.

Carlos Pouso, ex-coach of UD Logroñés referred to Guardiola's Barça, on the 5th of December of 2014, as follows: "Here nobody lets you play. Forget about it… This is turning into a sort of "philosophy of the game". I hear players talk about their way of playing and, funnily, when they play against my side I don't see it: playing from the back, combination play… We have to cut out the nonsense. That Barça of Guardiola has done a lot of harm to football because they played so wonderfully well that now there are lots of imitators that are a disaster. For my liking, this Barça plays very well and Real Madrid are fantastic. Now it seems that if you don't do rondos in your own box, even when losing 0-3, you don't play football. My team will keep playing without doing rondos in our box."

---

[1] It is important to highlight the opinion of Guardiola about the term 'tiki-taka'. He has said, "I hate 'tiki-taka'. I hate it. Tiki-taka is to pass the ball for the sake of it, with no intention. And that is useless. Don't believe what they say. Barça had nothing of tiki-taka! That's an invention! Ignore it!" Taken from p149 of 'Herr Pep', the book written by Martí Perarnau exploring Pep Guardiola's first year at Bayern Munich.

He continued, "Teams that ask center backs to play out without any sort of mechanism, teams that play 1–4–3–3 where the distance between lines is huge, teams that, in their eagerness to keep possession, play horizontally or even backwards until they lose the ball. Like that again and again. Teams that play rondos during training sessions without any transference to their model of play. Teams that do drills with one or two touch limits, minimizing the decision-making capacities of the player… a cluster of nonsense… consequences of Touch! Touch! Touch!"

Guardiola's approach involves remarkable challenges in technical execution and high complexity in the holistic interpretation of the model of play. This book is about more than the specific features of the Pep Team and the direct link to the group of players he had under him; it is about the *Pep Dream*. It is to be understood as the 'system of interactions' that create a collective behavior. As a consequence, coaches who try to get their teams practicing Guardiola's style of play without backing it up with a clear and detailed model of play will simply sink. Those teams are the caricatures of the Pep Team that have proliferated in the last few years with very little effect.

Can you play like Pep's Team without players as technically gifted as Xavi, Iniesta or Piqué?

Yes. Without a shadow of a doubt. However, it is also true that a minimum playing capacity in team members is needed to develop this model of play, although you *can* play the Pep way with players of medium abilities. It is also true to say that by playing the Pep way, players' progress will accelerate, and their overall technical capacities will grow. In turn, the cognitive capacities of players and the commitment of the squad to the plan will be key variables in the learning process and how quickly things can come together for you.

This document seeks to gather Guardiola's model of play at Barça – structured in Principles, Subprinciples, and Sub-Subprinciples – to plan the acquisition of these elements during preseason and to present a methodological framework in the context of Tactical Periodization.

While the book only covers preseason, it will lay out how the regular season is simply a continuation of everything we learn and implement. Training in the regular season is simply a furtherance of what we establish in preseason, tweaked based on the playing schedule and other resources at your disposal.

The four seasons that Guardiola spent in charge of the first team at Barça witnessed extraordinary richness and tactical variety. Every few months you could observe the team reinventing itself on the blackboard and on the field. That's why I wanted to choose the 2009-2010 Barça vintage; although subsequent teams maintained identical key principles, this was the best team to explore, in this book, with regard to technical demands. It was also the last season when 1-4-3-3 was the predominant system at Barça and the first when Lionel Messi's role as center forward became permanent and pivotal.

Play Like Pep Guardiola's Barcelona: A Soccer Coach's Guide is a title that aims to provoke the reader; taking aim at the ingenious attempts of many to imitate or copy the genius that is Pep, often without understanding the complexity of the tactical revolution that is involved. This book intends to thoroughly analyze the model of play of Pep's Team, and to present a methodological training framework that can be put into practice with a grassroots, amateur, or semi-professional team. Let's get started!

Model of Play

History and Background

Pep Guardiola once called himself a "thief of ideas." However, I prefer to see him like a 'chef.' Akin to the great chefs in history, he went to the market, meticulously chose each of his ingredients and – once in his kitchen – prepared the dish that he had dreamed about for so long: "the Pep Dream."

Let's have a quick look at the market stalls that Guardiola visited as he sought out his ingredients.

We have to go all the way back to Jany van der Veen, Ajax youth coach, and discoverer of Johan Cruyff, to begin to see the first traces of what would become positional play. Under van der Veen, 'immediate pressure' after losing the ball was a distinguishing mark of his teams in the Ajax academy in the late 60's.

Rinus Michels – Mr. Marble – manager of the Dutch national side at the 1974 World Cup in Germany, demonstrated a constant interchange of positions and a pressing defensive zone, transforming the way of playing soccer. He called it "play," the football universe wisely called it "total football."

It was 1990 when a young and skinny midfielder – Josep Guardiola – was called into the Barcelona first team, managed at the time by Johan Cruyff. Six subsequent years of living, talking, and training carved his character and gave him a most privileged way of understanding the game. The third man, width, pace, constant support and the rational occupation of space are some examples of what that historical "Dream Team" was all about. Guardiola was Cruyff's best example of a Dream Team player.

Later on, during his career at Barça, another master of positional play arrived… Louis van Gaal. There is no doubt that Pep, whilst maturing as a player, was further able to carry on collecting knowledge about tactics and training methodologies whilst working under the Dutchman. Van Gaal, the new tenant of the culé bench, had been manager of the European champions in 1995 with a very young Ajax side, always structured in triangles in his 3-4-3 playing system that enabled the team to build up long periods of possession. Van Gaal advocated patience to find the necessary space to arrive at goal, either from the sides or through the middle. One of his favorite sayings was, "I don't train for the legs, I train for the brain."

The contribution of Barça Manager Frank Rijkaard on the club's Model of Play is also important. Guardiola's predecessor instilled essential aspects to the team such as becoming organized through possession of the ball, and the extraordinary "6 seconds of pressure" (when Barcelona would press at full speed for 6 seconds after losing possession in the opposition's half).

Maybe the secret ingredient in the Guardiola recipe, however, comes from Pep's experience in Mexican football. Juan Manuel Lillo, coach (in 2005) of the still-playing Guardiola for the Mexican Dorados de Sinaloa side, is an accomplice to Pep in seeing the game as a constant search for spatio-temporal advantages. Ideas such as *"Positional Play consists of generating superiority behind the pressing line. Everything is much easier when the progress of the ball is clean."* are the genesis of the model of play that amazed the world.

Not quite happy with all the ingredients detailed, and keen to complete his menu, Guardiola also added a pinch of Sacchi, a bit of Menotti, a teaspoon of la Volpe and the always inspiring scent of Bielsa.

The table is set.

Model of Play versus Style of Play

There is certain confusion amongst analysts as to the terms 'style of play' and 'model of play'. The style of play refers to the descriptive manner in which a team plays, and can be broken down into three depending on the features of the *attacking moment*:

1. Combination style of play (a short passing game)
2. Direct style of play (a long passing game)
3. Counterattacking style of play (compact defending and the launching of quick runs/combinations when gaining possession of the ball)

Besides these three elements being rather broad, and also incorporating teams with very different models of play, we must take into account that the style of play is a label with limited tactical content. Guardiola's Barça used a 'combination style of play' but its way of playing was very different to other teams that used the combination style at the time.

The difference between styles of play is easily visible when comparing Pep's Barça with other teams that also aimed to play a combination style of play (such as Arsene Wenger's Arsenal, for example). Pep's approach was not primarily about short passes. It was not about moving the ball with pace. It was not about having possession. It was about dismembering the opposition at every pass. It was about building advantages at every interaction.

The model of play, however, captures the *details* of how a team plays across *specific contexts,* in the five moments of the game plus all of their sub-phases and beyond:

1. organized attack

2. organized defense
3. the transition from attack to defence
4. the transition from defence to attack
5. set pieces

The model of play also incorporates tactical variations based on the superiority or inferiority of the number of players, or the game's score.

Unai Emery, the former Sevilla manager and current manager of Paris Saint-Germain, maintains that no two models of play are the same. The football manager Oscar Cano goes even further saying that a team's playing model varies from week to week, even without the manager wanting it to, due to context and individual players. Both are right. It is possible to extract common behavioral patterns in a team in a fixed period. In fact, it is essential to synthesize a given model of play into Principles, Subprinciples, and Sub-Subprinciples in order to train it and grow through it.

The model established by Cruyff, developed by Van Gaal, used by Lillo to innovate, and improved by Guardiola, came to be called "El Juego de Posición" or "Positional Play." Each of these managers developed it with their own idiosyncrasies, with modifications year after year, and influence from the club environments where they coached. A core idea was maintained throughout, however: organization through the use of the ball.

Structure of Positional Play under the Model of Play

"The purpose of the rondo should be for the players in the middle not to get the ball, not for the ones outside not to lose it. I talk about solidarity, about creating spaces. Positional play. The purpose must be for the teammate to receive the ball with time and space. It's about delivering the ball. I don't give it until I have brought my opponent near me. In basketball, you always do this. Otherwise you are dead." Juanma Lillo

Plato, the philosopher, would say that positional play belongs to the world of ideas. He would also say that is difficult to find a unique definition or interpretation for it. It is true that the Pep team's way of playing became iconic as a system of interactions. It is also true that Guardiola showed the world that it was not like that; the system and the players did not matter, the only relevant thing was (and still is) *what* you play for.

Our analysis of the work of Guardiola at Barcelona has allowed us to examine the importance of the manager in the process. Once Pep stopped being team manager, the model of play he developed at Barça dissolved bit by bit, game after game. The tactical intensity faded. Indeed, in the last few years (although the team has still done well) there has been a drift in the way players play – at a personal as well as team level. It has affected the Barça game and its competitive ability but also the future of Spanish football.

Many supporters, as well as coaches, think that the priority of positional play is to keep possession. They confuse the means with the aim. Possession is, in fact, just the tool. The objective is to *dominate space*; hence the name "positional play" and not "possession play".

"Space is our compass and the Ball is our Oxygen"

The main idea behind positional play is to generate spatio-temporal advantages (i.e. advantages in a team's *space on the pitch* or their *time on the ball*) through the use of the ball. The opposition, ultimately, becomes disorganised as the ball is moved around – but it also becomes very easy to recover the ball if you lose it. In turn, being successfully counter-attacked by the opposition becomes very difficult. This is the truly revolutionary idea, the real identity of the idea that culminated in Barça's aims of 70% possession, 5-0 at half time, and 6 seconds of pressure.

Guardiola's model of play structure for set pieces was also revolutionary but maybe not as obvious. For instance, he sought to defend wide-angle free kicks from outside the box, to assist the goalkeeper and make finishing difficult. It was also characteristic for his teams to play short corners so they could attack through open play that did not necessarily require a conventional cross into the box.

To see the structure and training of the model of play in set pieces, see the Planning section.

Definitions and Explanations of Each Concept

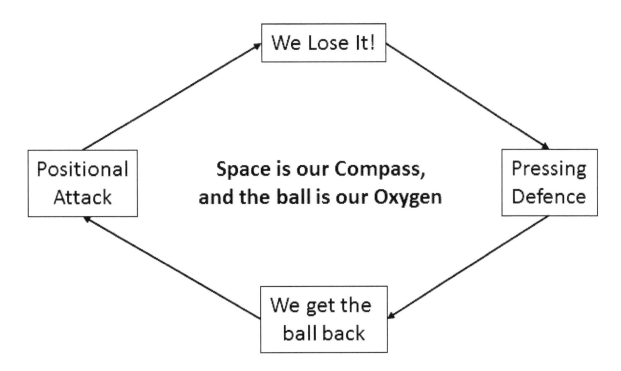

The true Macroprinciple that guides the various phases of the game is "Space is our compass and the ball is our oxygen", a phrase which offers a clear indication of what our team is trying to achieve. Having possession of the ball is an imperative, whilst creating space in order to arrive at goal finishing situations is the main objective.

The idiosyncrasies of the model of play will be defined by how players interpret the model, and the relations that arise between them. However, the group must have a single (unitary) response to each trigger in the game. To do that, playing gets structured into a series of Principles, SubPrinciples and Sub-Subprinciples depending on the moment of the game we are at.

The model of play is defined, as mentioned previously, by the moments of the game that correspond to:

1. when we have the ball
2. when we lose it
3. when we don't have it
4. when we get it back
5. each time we face a set piece (offensive or defensive)

In the organized attack of the Pep Team, the priority was positional attack that was guided by the following principles:

1. Moving together as the ball advanced
2. Generating spacio-temporal advantages

Positional Attack

Key:

| Principle | Sub-Principle | Sub-Sub principle |

Travelling with the ball			
Numerical Superiority	Rational Occupation of Space	Pace of Play	Patience/Continuity
Dribbling to release	Relational distances	Offensive building timing	
Constant support	Receivers at different lengths of pass	Support behind the line of the ball	
Adding players from other lines	Width		
	Depth		
	Secure possession zone		

For positional attack, we shall dig a little deeper and cover each Principle, Subprinciple and Sub-Subprinciple.

Principle: Travelling with the ball

In the same way that a painter needs his canvas and paints to carry out his artwork, the footballer needs the ball. For that to happen, the most basic thing is to *hold on to possession and not lose it*. This will increase the chances of scoring a goal and, in consequence, get a team closer to victory. To be able to achieve this principle, we will need to use different Subprinciples, which will contain Sub-Subprinciples that will help us to develop our game.

Subprinciple: Numerical superiority

We must always try to have more of our players in zones that are proximal to the ball. In this way, we increase our chances of retaining possession.

Sub-Subprinciple: Driving the ball to release it

Driving with the ball at your feet, on most occasions, acts as a magnet for the opposition who are trying to regain it. Thus, driving with the ball will allow teammates to be released from their markers or provide enough space to connect a pass to them. In quantitative terms, it is all about creating a 2v1 where there was previously a 1v1.

Sub-Subprinciple: Constant support

Logic tells us that if football is a team sport, and taking into account that we want to keep possession for as long as possible, we need the participation of all our players. It's essential for the man in possession to always have 2 or 3 options when passing the ball, and this is what we mean by constant support. There has been a lot of talk about the "triangles" drawn by a team, but a complete set of support goes further than a triangle – it consists of one or two lateral support options), support ahead of the ball, and one or two safety options (i.e. support behind the ball). It is *not* a triangle, not even a diamond, we could say is an inverted neck tie.

Triangle

Diamond

Inverted neck-tie

Sub-Subprinciple: Adding players from other lines

A full-back advancing a few metres into the midfield line, or a midfielder coming down between the center-backs into the defense's line, makes ball recovery difficult for an opponent because, most probably, these movements create a numerical advantage in certain areas of the field.

Sub-Principle: Rational occupation of space

Football has more in common with chess than you may think; teams operate to threaten the rival king and, at the same time, protect their own. This way, each individual movement requires a collective re-balancing of positions that keep our team's positions stable, and which provides advantages to deliver strikes against the opponent. There is only a slight difference; in chess, you move one piece at a time, and there are 64 squares. In football 22 players move simultaneously, and there is an infinite range of positions available. That is why it is key to occupy the board (i.e. the pitch) in a rational and balanced way.

Sub-Subprinciple: Relational distances

Basically, depth and width. It is important to create support behind, and in front of, the opposition's line of pressure so that we can move the ball without jeopardising the passing line. In other words, team mates must not be too close together or too far apart. If the first option happens, there is an accumulation of opposition players and very little space to execute actions correctly. The second one is just as harmful because, as you might find on a ladder, climbing one step at a time is easy, but taking two rungs at once gets complicated, and climbing three rungs at once is almost impossible. So, let's do things easily, and take one step or rung at a time. Each step is a level or crossways section of the pitch; the more lines we form, the more rungs are made available for a safe climb.

Sub-Subprinciple: Receivers at different lengths of pass

If we position ourselves in a stepped way – within levels of the pitch – we can achieve a positional advantage that enables us to progress and get closer to the opposition goal to score.

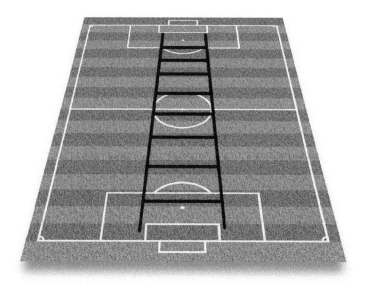

Think about the pitch as though it has a ladder laid over it. Each rung or step on the ladder takes the play (and the team) up to the next level of the pitch, towards the opposition's goal. Thus, as we step up onto each rung, we progress up the pitch. The narrow ladder (above) is just to help visualise the concept. In reality, it is as wide as the pitch.

Sub-Subprinciple: Width

Making life difficult for the opposition's defence and its recovery of the ball are our objectives. Full-backs and wingers hugging the sidelines make the pitch too wide to defend comfortably.

Sub-Subprinciple: Depth

A vulnerable space for the opposition is the back of their defensive line. With through-balls, we can threaten the space in behind defenders. This causes opposing players to drop off to protect this space. Therefore, we now have enough space to keep possession of the ball and make a "step up the ladder".

Sub-Subprinciple: Secure possession zone

Xavi Hernández recognized in the book "Champions Path" (by Marti Perarnau) how, at la Masia, they taught him that the key was *not to lose the ball*. Keeping possession in order to climb our proverbial ladder is basic, and players have to secure each zone where we have the ball. Support *behind* any player with the ball is essential to provide options for the man in possession, as well as providing cover and an immediate press should possession be lost. It is also important that the ball always goes to zones of numerical superiority. If we orientate our possession to a zone where we are outnumbered or find ourselves positionally disadvantaged, we endanger possession and our 'one rung at a time' protocol.

The ball must move quickly, passes must be focused with touches kept to a minimum (i.e. one touch, or control and pass). Dynamic and lively possession will allow us to throw the opposition off balance, inhibit their recovery time, and often offer us a way to find subsequent advantage. Changing the pace of play suddenly is also important (e.g. passing slowly then suddenly playing a quick, incisive pass) to exploit the opposition when they are disorganized or out of balance.

Sub-Subprinciple: Offensive temporization

The player with the ball is directly responsible for collective positioning. He has to provide the time needed for teammates to spread out and step up together. Either with a sideways dribble or by putting together a couple of short passes with a teammate, he will give the team those necessary seconds to achieve depth and positional balance.

Sub-Subprinciple: Support behind the line of the ball

Back to our imaginary ladder, but this time with a twist. Imagine how – as we climb every rung or step – it disappears! It's a ladder that creates panic! We need the security that the step below gives us, so it's key that players are present and able to receive the ball behind the player in possession. We must always have safe options in case a forward advance is not possible.

Something we need to understand fully is how our type of play sees rivals accumulate lots of players in the defensive area. If we fall into the trap of rushing our decision-making, we will make mistakes that shorten our period in possession. In essence, we will fall halfway down the ladder time and time again. So, we must remain patient and keep doing what our model of play dictates.

Creating Space

Creating Space			
Find the Free Man	Width and Depth	Interchange of Positions	Third Man
Dribbling to release		Incorporation of the first line	
Pace of play with near players		Movements to break from the second line	
Attract opposition to free up other players		Support movements of the third line	

Principle of Attack: Creating Space

We have the ball but what do we do with it? On a pitch with 22 players, a referee, and a space where offside exists, we generate our own spaces or we may run out of playing space. We will make use of a few Subprinciples and Sub-Subprinciples to generate those spacio-temporal (space and time) advantages that we need.

Sub-Principle: Finding the free man

We are 11, and so are they. A free man? Impossible? Nothing could be further from the truth. There is always someone free of their marker (or removed enough to recognize himself as the free man) who can ask for the ball and find himself in a good position to play it. Finding the next free man (including the goalkeeper) is the key for our positional game.

Sub-Subprinciple: Dribbling to release

Similar to the idea expressed earlier… I have the ball, does an opponent want it? Come and try to get it. While you are coming, I am sure one of my teammates will find the free space that you have left behind.

Sub-Subprinciple: Pace of play with proximal players

We look to move the ball as quickly as possible when passing it to a close teammate, and get it to a teammate before the opposition reduces his space.

Sub-Subprinciple: Attract to free up further players

Positional play *does not* reject long passes. However, you need to create width or depth advantages to secure success and generate time and space for the receiver. You can do this by scattering rival players by making close passes or dribbles that cause them to gravitate towards the ball. In doing so, you will create space in other parts of the pitch, especially in areas far away from the ball.

Placing midfielders or wingers right on the touchline is no whim. Such positions open up a world of possibility for attacking the rival goal. The wider your team plays, the wider the opposition is tempted to defend, and, as a result, internal corridors will show up for sure.

If the opposition advances their defensive line a lot (in order to prevent us having comfortable possession), we must force them to retreat more often than they would like to. A few deep passes behind the defense will cause them to lose confidence. We know that human beings are vulnerable when they feel at risk. Opposition players will prefer to find a way to feel comfortable, and that will allow us to have possession in more advantageous situations.

Rotation between players of different positions and lines adds a touch of dynamism and creates surprise for our rivals. These interchanging movements are capable of putting all marking systems in jeopardy.

Sub-Subprinciple: Incorporation of the first line

Defenders tend to avoid circulating the ball once it has left the first pressure zone, but it is key (if we want to keep on creating numerical superiority) that they get into the habit of being a useful passing option. At times, they will have to join in the theoretical line (or grouping) of midfield.

Sub-Subprinciple: Movements to break from the second line

The positional attack of this model of play implies that opponents will often defend deep, making it difficult for the team in possession to get 'in behind' the team's defence. Opening spaces behind the deep defensive line is only possible with forward runs and movements from wingers and even midfielders.

Sub-Subprinciple: Support movements of the third line

A lot has been said of the "false 9", but false 7s and 11s (wingers who come and play inside such as Messi as right wing in Guardiola´s first two seasons, or Iniesta when placed on the left wing), by comparison, have remained fairly anonymous. An example might be the striker that joins the midfield but who doesn't avoid his duties in the box. As Pep said: it's more lethal to *arrive* into the box than to be there.

A concept with the stamp of La Masia on it. Guardiola said that Cruyff always told him "When you have the ball, always look at Romario. If he has space to receive the ball, we give it to him and then get close to him, he will always play to a forward-running midfielder who will receive it behind their markers."

Attacking Transition

For the sake of brevity, subsequent Principles, Sub-Principles and Sub-Subprinciples will be listed in table form only. Here is the table for attacking transition:

Attacking Transition	
Use Free Spaces	Timing of Offensive Buildup Play
Pace of play. Speed of circulation.	*Safe technical action*
Numerical superiority from the third man	*Keep the ball*
Finishing	*Rational occupation of space*

Defending

The defensive phase of Pep's Barça is difficult to analyze because it rarely appears and – even then – only for short periods of time each game. The *predominant* defensive moment is not the organized defense but the transition from attack to defense, and it would be rather adventurous to define the behaviors that rule such a brief moment. Understanding the controversy of such an analysis, however, I propose a synthesis of the Pressing Defense of Pep's Barça through the following Principles and Subprinciples, in each of the subphases.

Pressing Defense			
Zonal Marking	Defend higher up the pitch	Press and Screen	Defensive Depth
Hounding the opposition if they have the ball.	Defensive timing. Prevent advance.	Screen my direct opponent's passing line	Reduce space in depth
Vigilance without the ball	Advance as the opposition passes back or when turned opponents have the ball	Hound the ball carrier	Reduce space in width
Covering the nearby zone, building up a defensive triangle with the hounding man	Watch our backs, move sideways		Build up defensive line density

Defensive Transition

Where did we lose the ball?

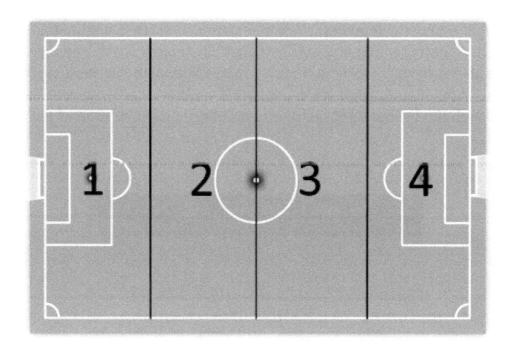

Can I press?

How many passes did we make in the lost possession zone?

A – More than 3, press in that zone

B – Less than 3, pressing retreat in next zone back

Attitude after losing the ball	
Pressing [get ready to press the opposition collectively in order to have a defensive numerical superiority]	Drop off [a player delays opponent's advance whilst the remainder of the team reorganize to prevent play progressing]
Set marking responsibilities	
Screen lines of pass	
Generate defensive numerical superiority	

Defensive Tactical Intensity

Tito Ramallo, one of the most prolific coaches of the Galician school, suggests a classification that can help to differentiate each of the ways a team may defend. Under the concept of Defensive Tactical Intensity[2], he establishes the following table, referring to how *a team* defends.

		Attitude towards the ball		
		Passive	Marking	Tackle
	Compact	1	4	5
Positioning	Expanded	2	6	7
	Spread Out	3	8	9

The two variables that the classification establishes are: defensive positioning (compact, expanded, spread out), and the attitude of defenders towards players with the ball (passive, actively marking opponents, getting tackles in). The number refers to the intensity of the defensive collective action with 1 being the lowest and 10 being the highest.

---

[2] Ramallo, Tito. "Medición De La Intensidad Táctica Defensiva (ITD)." Http://www. futbolofensivo.com. Javier Lavandera, 4 Nov. 2013. Web. 7 Apr. 2015.

There is a third (unseen) variable, too. It's the variable that takes a team from a defensive tactical intensity (DTI) of 9 to 10, and it's the number of covering players behind the line of the ball in the attacking phase. If a team leaves fewer than four men behind the ball and defends with an attitude that seeks to recover the ball, that team is defending with DTI 10.

The Barça of Guardiola was a team of DTI 10, probably the first I have seen which pressed across the whole pitch, over 90 minutes. They worked to prevent the opposition's first line from receiving the ball or playing. They generated defensive positioning with no fear of players abandoning the zone they were supposed to cover if it was necessary to create defensive numerical superiority in another zone where the ball was.

It is difficult to simplify, in a static zonal diagram, the distribution of the defensive responsibilities of Guardiola's team. It is also important to highlight that there was no retreat zone but an ambition to defend forwards. The team would press high up the pitch until they recovered the ball or, if their position was overrun, they had to run backwards to balance space and defend the box. Finally, we cannot forget that defensive operations would vary depending on the players lined up and their positions on the field. However, at the risk of losing credibility, allow me the audacity to simplify such a complex phenomenon into the following zonal diagram.

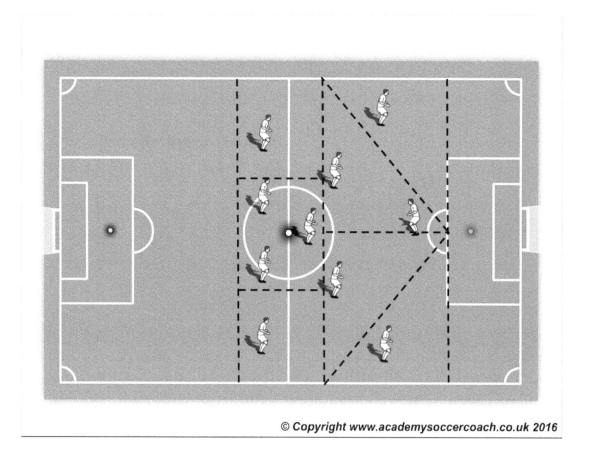

The height (up the pitch) of this pressing retreat could be even higher, putting the defensive line in the opposition's half and the first pressing line all the way to the penalty area. Of course, the height up the pitch to start the press depends on the position of the opposition's defenders and their attitude towards starting the play.

We establish seven pressing zones at the maximum convenient height up the pitch. Six field players will have a preferential defending zone and four will have the following complementary behaviors. The zones will set pressing responsibilities and collective behavioral patterns.

Specifics:

- The two center backs have a common area assigned; when one of them presses, the other one must cover and, in certain circumstances, both can go for the ball. Additionally, one of the center backs will be in charge of covering any space that gets generated behind full backs who have left their zone to create an offensive or defensive numerical superiority.
- The defensive midfielder has no assigned zone; instead, he will cover the opposition player on the pressing line in front of him. Also, at the risk of the opponent playing long, he can prioritize defending the area guarded by the center backs when facing teams who do not play on the inside.
- The striker presses freely, without thinking about things too much, covering mainly the passing lines to the central midfielder and remaining alert for a possible offensive transition when the ball is won back.

Another main feature of this diagram is with how much frequency and aggression the full-backs press up the pitch; they may press right up behind the midfielders.

What do we need for our team to have a DTI of 9?

For a DTI of 9, we need the following four principles to underpin the defensive phase of the model of play:

1. Zonal marking with aggression towards the player with the ball.
2. Gain defensive height up the pitch.
3. Pressing and screening that leads to defensive numerical superiority.
4. Defensive depth with aggressive, well-organised and committed players.

Nevertheless, we cannot forget that to be able to defend forwards (in an effective manner) you must have attacked through numerical superiority (travelling together) first. Only by attacking in that way will we achieve a rational occupation of the pitch that allows for a pressing defence. Otherwise, by the time pressure arrives (a matter of seconds) the opposition (which has suffered little disorder because few players have pressed) will already have played a pass to the back of the defence.

Specifics of Guardiola's defence in the Zone of Pressure

What to do when I have two players in my zone and one of them has the ball?

© Copyright www.academysoccercoach.co.uk 2016

Example of zonal marking of a team that defends 1-4-3-3 (white) representing Pep's team, against a team that attacks with a 1-4-2-3-1 (black).

For some time (since Arrigo Sacchi's time) the dominant tactic (in the case of the graphic with two opponents in the ball zone) has been for the defending team to get positioned in front of the player with the ball, at the same level as his teammate (or a couple of metres behind), to control the situation while waiting for help. It is obvious that this is not a zonal pressing defence (due to the passive attitude of the defender). In the case of the white right winger in the example, he is not able to pressure the left black center back because he has another opponent in his zone.

The zonal marking press of Guardiola's model, however, demands that pressure be active by creating positional numerical superiority in the pressing area. So while we wait for help to arrive (teammates will come to press and screen… to create numerical superiority) the ideal movements from the player must be:

1) run to screen the line of pass between the two opposition players and

2) run towards the player with the ball to force him to get rid of the ball or execute a defensive technical action.

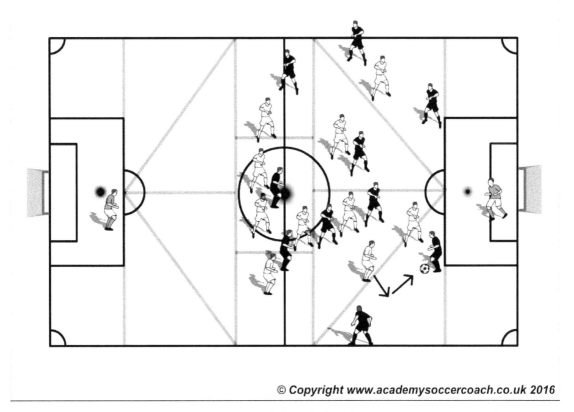

Example of the behavior of the defender to gain positional superiority despite numerical inferiority.

On paper, everything works, but what happens if the pressing player (or any other) gets outpaced in the pressing zone? In such a case, players from adjacent zones (that were already getting close) will jump to follow the same procedure: 1) run to screen the line of pass 2) press on the run.

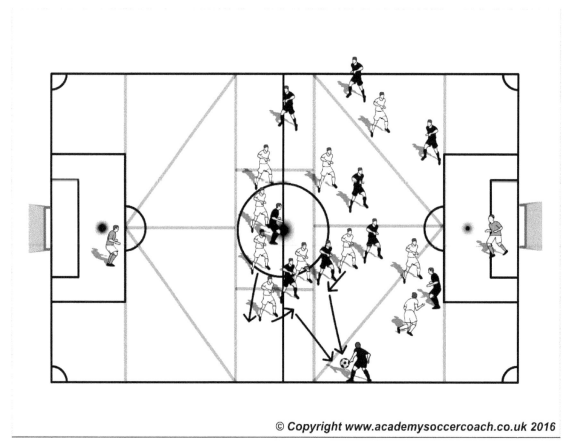

Example of assisting behavior, sent to obtain defensive numerical superiority or support for the outpaced teammate.

For the pressing defence to be effective, the players must anticipate the development of the play in order to generate continual positional superiority that will, in turn, bring defensive numerical superiority.

When the first pressing line and its covering players (midfielders, wingers and pivot) gets overrun, the whole team should retreat to a level where the line formed by the wingers and midfielders is behind the ball and the zonal pressing process may restart.

To slow down the progression of the opposition team and allow the defence to get reorganised, the defensive timing of the players covering the first line of pressure will be very important. If is not possible to restructure the defensive block in time, the priority is to organize a structure to defend the box with the first players to retreat.

The Attack-Defence transition is a key and inextricable part of the offensive moment since it starts to form during the organized attack.

Patience when in possession, while the team advances together, will result in numerical superiority around the ball when possession is lost; while support behind the ball will facilitate effective pressure after losing possession. In turn, the disorder that is created against the opposition will handicap their offensive transition.

So, before any loss of possession, much will depend on whether the team has travelled together to the zone where the ball has been lost. If this has been accomplished, the team will press aggressively generating defensive numerical superiority through press and screen, and move the defensive block forward. The aim will be to regain possession within 6 seconds.

If we didn't travel together (or the opposition manages to survive the first 6 seconds of pressure) then we perform a retreat to the zone behind where the ball was lost, and a "zonal pressing defence" (as detailed in the Organized Defence section) is initiated. During the Guardiola years, there was also a tactic, deployed during the defensive transition, whenever it was impossible to recover the ball immediately. If the opposition overcame the immediate defensive pressure, one of the wingers would commit a tactical foul to allow the team to retreat. Because the opposition were not in a position to initiate meaningful progress up the pitch towards goal, the chances of getting a yellow card were minimal.

The Defence to Attack transition is a key moment of Pep's Playing Model since it's the point at which to decide which type of attack is most effective. If we rob the opposition of the ball at a moment when they are disorganized, we will take advantage of the space generated and attack through the following Subprinciples:

1. Pace of play. Speed of circulation.
2. Numerical superiority involving three or more players (e.g. 3v2, 4v3, etc *not* 2v1) trying to outrun the opposition's reorganization using a third man combination.
3. Quick finishing, or back to an organized attack.

If, when regaining the ball, we notice that the opposition is well organized, leaving no space for an easy progression, we will perform an offensive temporization before moving on to the usual Positional Attack.

Offensive temporization:

1. A 'safety first' technical action
2. Keep possession of the ball
3. Rational occupation of space

Striving for the Model of Play… through Movement

In football, there are two primary schools when it comes to the concept of the model of play:

- The Portuguese school, based on the interrelation of Principles, Subprinciples, and Sub-subprinciples, for each of the phases and subphases of the game. As explained in the "The Model of Play" section, the perspective of Principles is the one I find more convenient. It transmits the model of play in a way that lets the player read the game, finding their own internal logic to our way of playing.
- The traditional school. It embraces the primary importance of having a model of play to guide the process of training and direction of the team. From the point of view of individual movements, they depend on the position of the player, teammates, the ball, and each of their rivals. To detail a model of play from this second perspective is a mammoth task due to the number of variables that need to be taken into account, and consequently the movements to memorize. However, it is a very enriching task because it captures answers for all possible situations.

In order to develop a model of play through movement, the first step is to divide the pitch into relevant areas so one can recognize different situations and define movements. As a commonly accepted protocol (and relevant to the movements required by this model of play in particular) we will divide the field into four horizontal zones (looking from one end of the pitch, running from goal to goal) and five vertical corridors.[3]

---

[3] This division is a simplification of the one Pep Guardiola requested to be painted on one of the pitches at Säbener Strasse (Bayern Munich training facilities) when he first arrived.

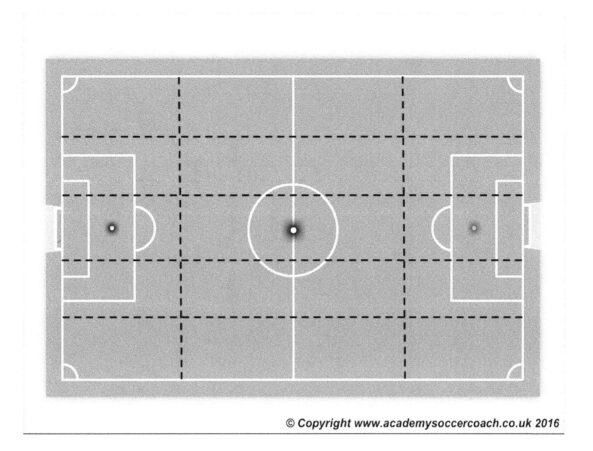

Once the pitch is divided, it is essential to establish a preferential system of play that will be the starting position for each movement and interaction. Before going into detail for each situation (depending on the position of the ball) it is advisable to establish a system and model of play for the opposition.

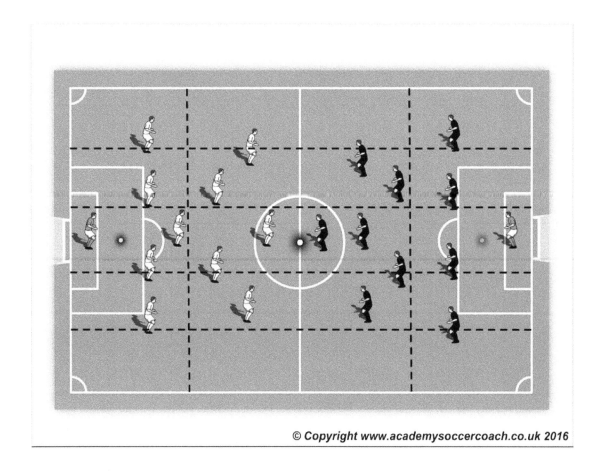

It is important to highlight that the above figures, and the figures in the upcoming illustrations, face different directions allowing us to establish an individual profile for each player (based on their field position and where they are looking); body position is a key aspect when it comes to having fast and effective circulation of the ball.

We have chosen a 1-4-3-3 (in white) as our formation (i.e. Pep's Barcelona) and a 1-4-2-3-1 (in black) for the opposition system; such a setup is one of the most common at all levels of football. In the following images, we will simulate the retreat of a team that defends through a middle block.

Approximation to the phase of organized attack

We will look at different snapshots of each team's movements in an organized attack from a goal kick. It is just an example and is only representative against one type of predetermined retreat, system, and defensive attitude. Also, it is necessary to highlight that positional play is an open model of play that does not pretend to automate movements; it just provides collective solutions so the player can choose an individual response, guided by common principles. So, each situation will allow a number of behaviors to be chosen from… in accordance with the model of play. For the sake of clarity, here are the positions that the following section refers to:

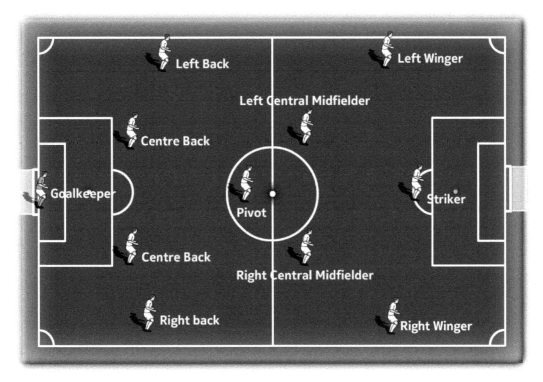

Taking into account that only one of the infinite possibilities of play (in accordance with the model of play) is represented in each graphic, the following analysis is a useful way to exemplify the movements and positions of a Guardiola's team's positional attack. The following behaviors have special emphasis.

1. Driving the ball or dribbling to release.
2. Numerical superiority.
3. Constant support. Creating "inverted neck-ties" (the evolution of triangles and diamonds).
4. Defensive timing each time a zone higher up the pitch is conquered (to get closer again).
5. Midfielder movements to stabilize space, depending on which corridor the ball is in.
6. Winger movements to stabilize space, depending on the depth of the ball.
7. Interactions between the three strikers to give width and depth whilst, at the same time, generating numerical superiority in the final third.
8. The natural tendency in this model is to start the play using inside corridors, before progressing the ball into outside ones. Then play is switched back in – to create numerical and positional advantages before outside diagonal runs lead to goal-bound finishes.

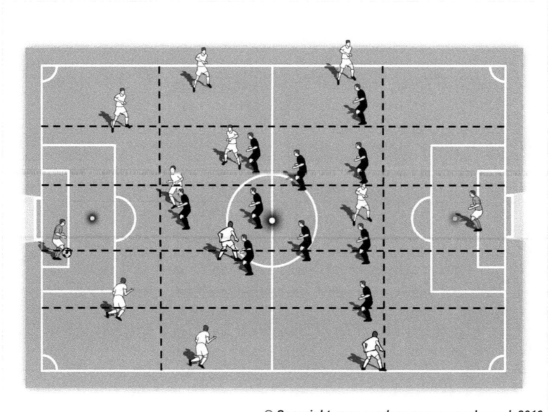

The three white attackers (striker and wingers) get positioned with depth and width to stretch the opposing team. The midfielders advance their position to be able to pass the first line of pressure if they receive a pass. The center backs stay open so they can receive the ball with space and time to play. The center midfielder holds his position because the opposing team is pressing the center backs through a lone striker. The wingers come close to the midfielder to give him support once the goalkeeper puts the ball into play.

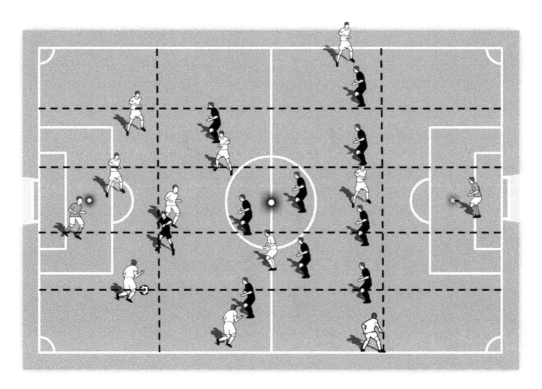

We will simulate that the pass chosen by the goalkeeper is to the right center back. The left center back will get closer to the player with the ball to offer a safe passing option. The left back will balance the space by leaving some room between himself and the sideline. The pivot, the right back, and the right central midfielder will form the diamond of support.

The opposing team has cut off all the passing options, but the right center back can dribble into the space given to free a teammate as we can see in the next snapshot.

31

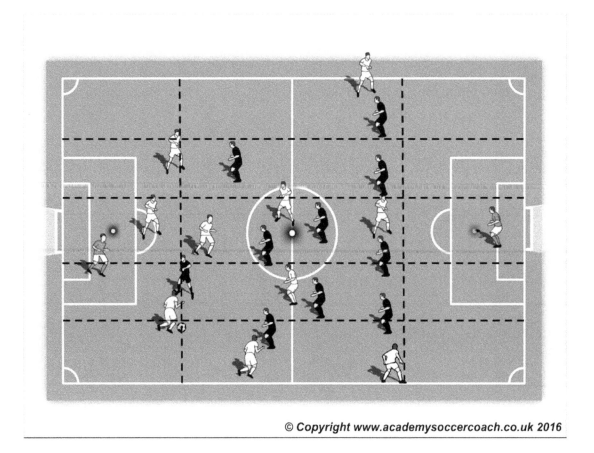

The pivot is freed but the passing line has not opened with him. As you can see in the next image, the center back can pass to the free man, using the passing line that he has with the right central midfielder.

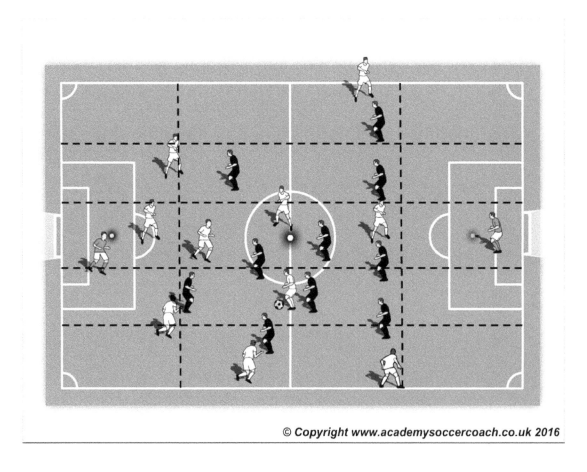

The receiver (right central midfielder), who is turned and with no advantage whatsoever, can pass the ball to the free man, who is nearby and facing him, executing what is called the 'third man'.

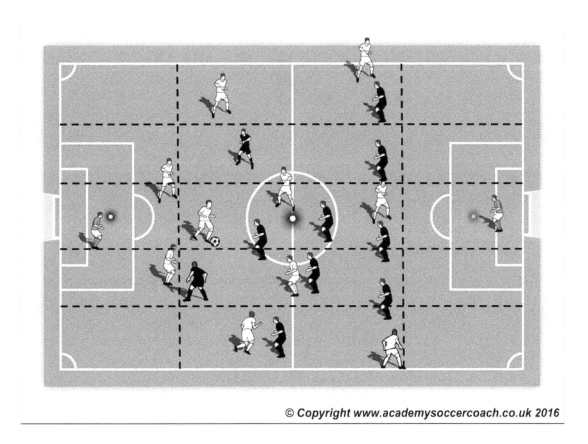

The new free man has several options (besides the safety pass offered by the left central back) as we can see from the diamond formed with the central midfielders and the striker (or the one formed with the left back, the left winger and the striker).

This second option is without a doubt a scenario with greater advantages than the first one. The player with more space and time to progress the play is the left back. Because a direct pass could put possession in danger, the ball is passed to him through the left central midfielder.

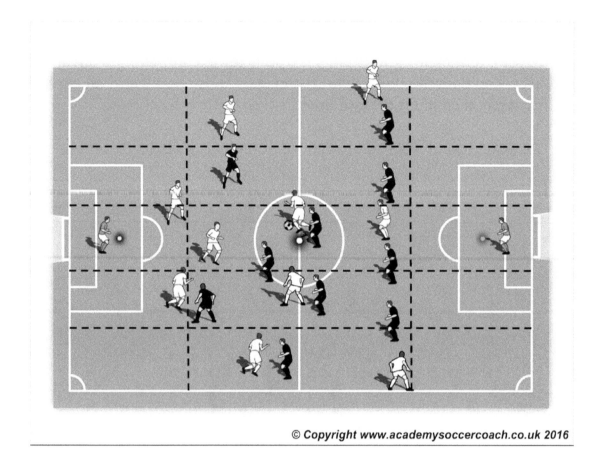

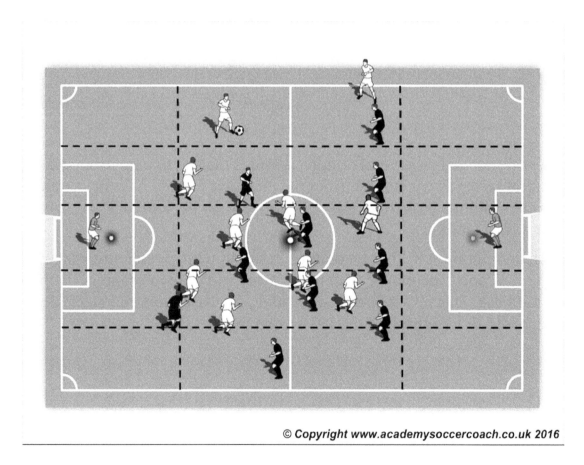

The left back is now in a position to dribble to progress, and free of some of his teammates ahead. However, he must juggle his intention to advance with the need for the team to 'travel together' and his teammates need time to occupy the necessary positions for mutual support and cooperation. Therefore, that 'dribble to release' must be in the form of offensive temporization.

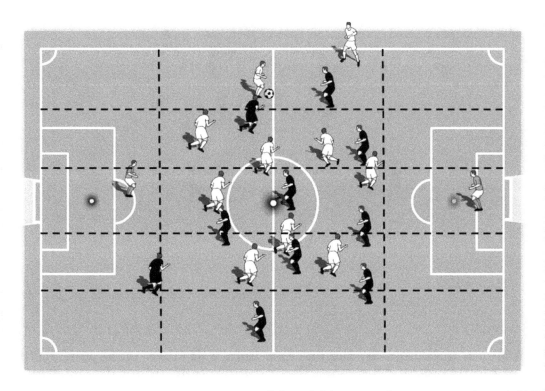

In the image, you can see how the team has taken advantage of the temporization to restructure and gain depth and at the same time the dribbling has attracted the attention of the opposition's right back, setting our own left winger free.

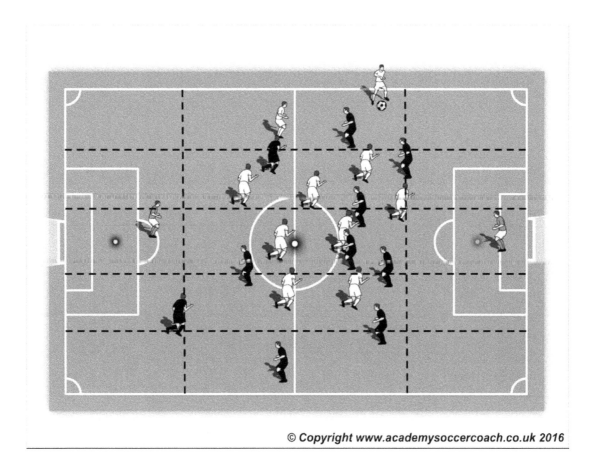

The receiving of the ball by the last line man will allow us to gain offensive depth and will push the defensive line to lose depth. When this happens, it provides time and space for our central midfielders to move behind the back of the opposition's second line.

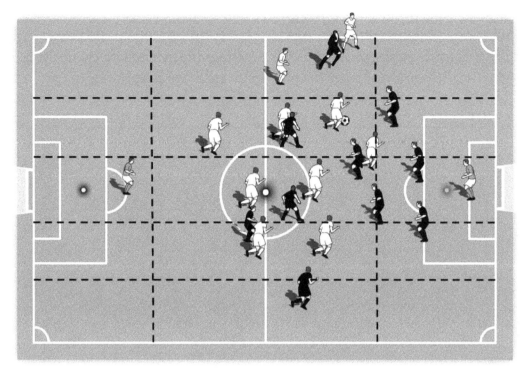

Once we are set in the third quarter of the pitch, it is essential for the team to be patient; this offers continuity to the play through generated numerical superiority.

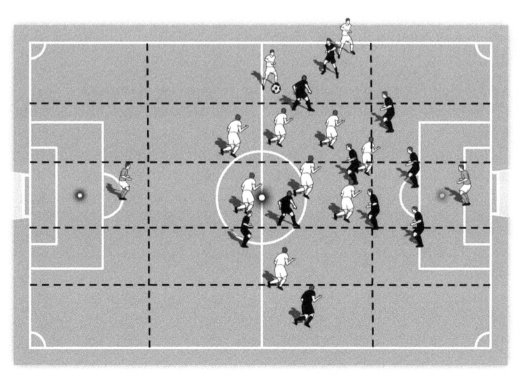

Besides becoming organized through the use of the ball (and disorganizing the opposition), this sequence of passes fulfils an objective of circulating the ball to the next relevant point that will produce numerical or positional superiority – allowing our team to penetrate into the last zone.

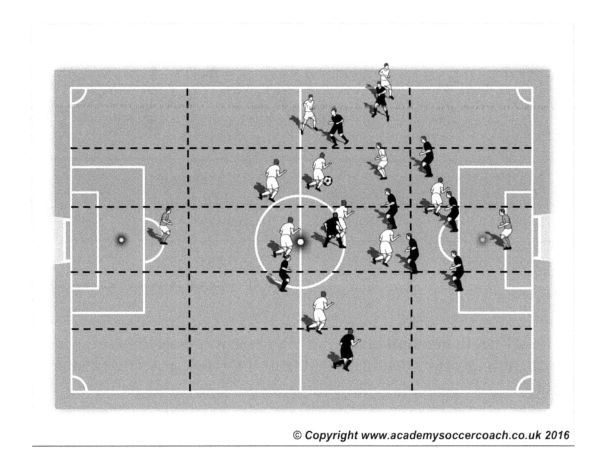

Let's remember that the three mechanisms (Sub-Subprinciples) for finding a free man are:

1. The pace of play (if you are playing with close teammates)
2. Dribbling to attract the marker of a nearby teammate, thus setting him free
3. Getting the attention of an opponent through a technical action in order to get the ball to a distant teammate

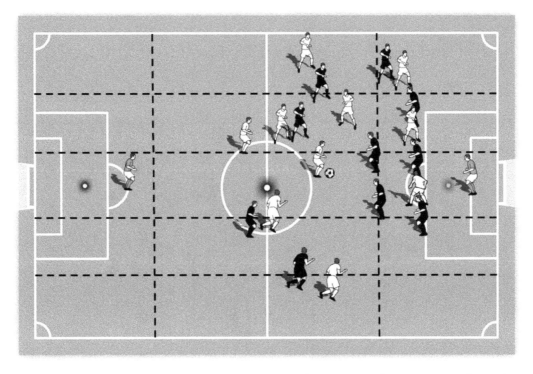

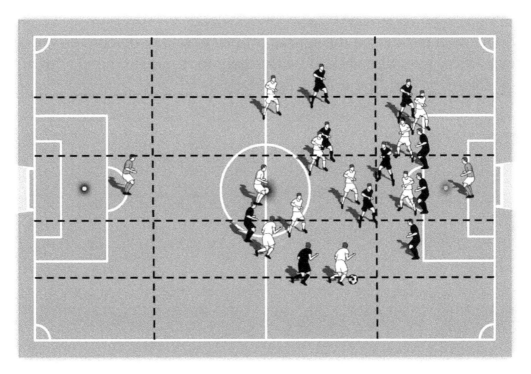

When an advantage presents itself, it must be used to overcome opposition pressure, and advance. However, an advantage in an advanced area does not mean that the advantage is certain and, accordingly, we should not rush the play.

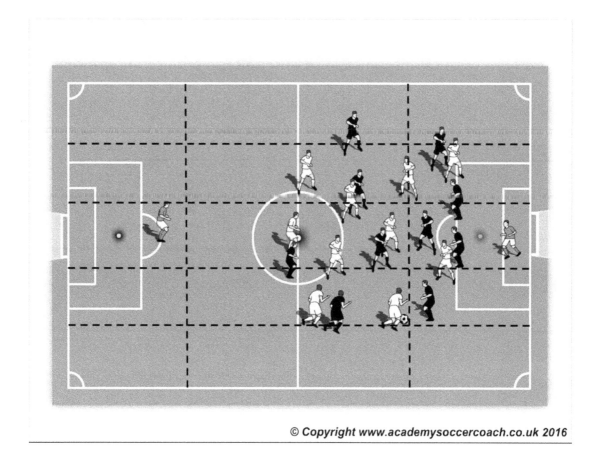

If the opposition has closed the spaces properly, it may be convenient to look for a safety pass that will allow the team to orientate the play to a corridor where we can find a fresh advantage.

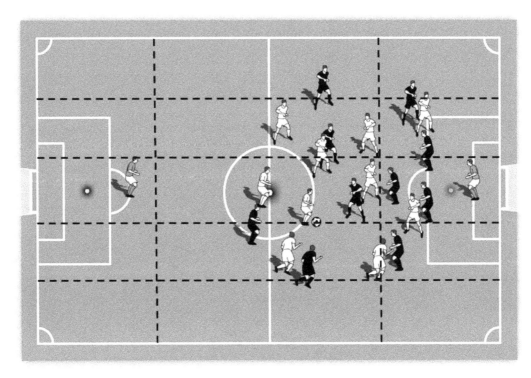

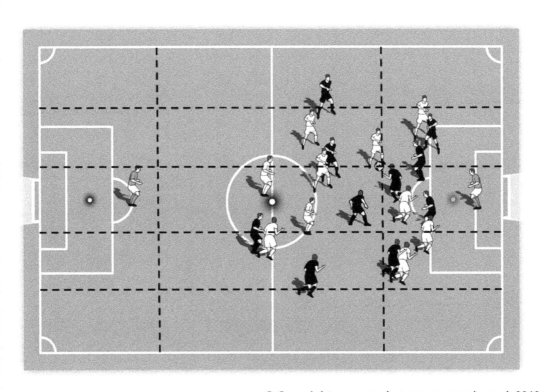

If our team manages to receive the ball with the central midfielder on the edge of the box (sitting behind the opposition's midfielders) – a quick combination and the arrival into the box of the three attackers can prove impossible to defend against.

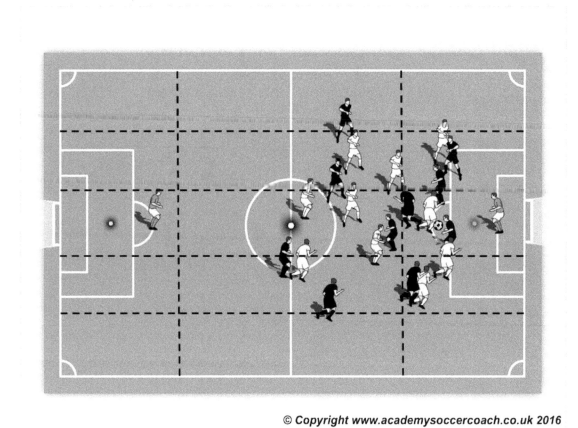

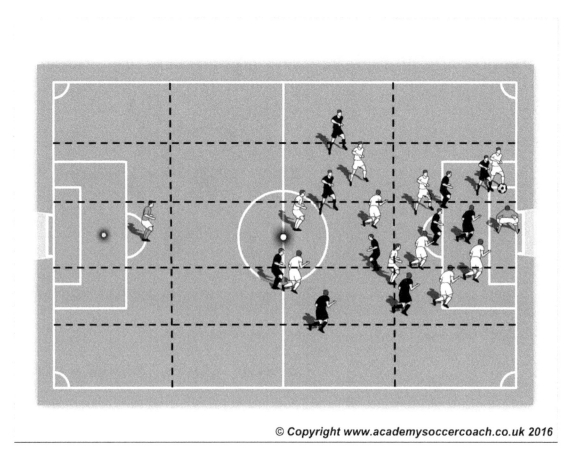

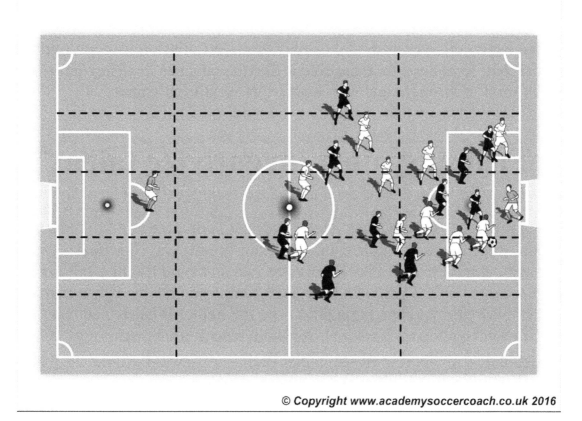

Pep's Team was unfairly characterised for approaching goal through give-and-gos, but (and this is independent to the technical excellence of their players) approaches were only possible thanks to the numerical and positional superiorities built in the last quarter of the pitch which were a result of much patience during progression. Once installed in the final zone, the speed the team put on the ball did the rest.

Methodological Framework

Once we have defined our model of play, our next mission is to get our team to embrace it; to believe in it and live it like the coaches do. They have to enjoy it, think it through, and above all *try it out* during games.

"Training must incentivize talent"

Training must focus on the way a team learns to compete and face every situation of the game in a joined-up (i.e. team-based) way. Tactical Periodization and Structuralist Theory are two systemic training schools that respect the unity of the game and see performance gains through a team's model of play [for detailed explanation see the book "What is Tactical Periodization" by Xavier Tamarit]. As such, below, a methodology comprising a large number of components from Tactical Periodization and a hint of structuralism will be offered.

The Task

The 'drill' is the tool that technical staff use to transmit a model of play to a team and, at the same time, is how players operationalise the model and live it as a team. It is not the only tool, of course, but it is the most powerful one.

Does this mean that tactical talks and blackboard sessions are of no use?

No. They may be useful as a means to communicate information to players, and to help them understand it. But, by themselves, they will never help a player get a 'feel' for what you are asking. They will never be able to create a collective subconscious that makes the team move as a single unit, or think and understand the game in the same way. Such sessions do not help players identify situations and apply collective solutions.

Should we burn down the blackboards? Should we eliminate the tactical talks?

No, definitely not. They are fantastic tools for bringing ideas together and visualizing static situations that help to understand the dynamic of the game.

Coming back to drills, they must be collective experiments. Coaches must present different scenarios to players with repetitive circumstances so they find collective, collaborative and simultaneous solutions. This type of approach is called 'guided discovery.'

Each task is centered around key factors that will define it, and by descriptive factors that will shape it.

Key Factors

- **Main objective:** working a particular Principle and/or Subprinciple of the model of play.
- **Level of difficulty:** how easy or difficult it will be to reach the objective. Parameters that condition difficulty:
  1 *Space.* The bigger the playing area, the less difficult the task.
  2 *Number of neutrals.* Greater numerical superiority, less difficulty.
  3 *Speed of circulation.* The faster the ball moves, the more difficult the task.
  4 *Restriction of stimuli.* Okay, asking your players to play with blindfolds may be unwise, but you can use earplugs to cut out auditory stimuli, or get everyone to wear the same strip to make visual identification more challenging.

- **Level of complexity:** this relates to the cognitive load of the drill, the number of variables that impact upon decision making.

1. Type of drill. Organized from low to high complexity:

1.1 Skill games

1.2 Analytical drills

1.3 Circuits

1.4 Rondos

1.5. Finishing games

1.6 Ball possession games

1.7 Position games

1.8 Small-sided games

1.9 Standard games

2. System/Positions. If the drill requires players to position themselves according to a particular tactical system, there is more complexity.

3. Lines. As the number of lines increases, the task will become progressively more complex.

4. Type of content. If the main objective is a Subprinciple, the drill will be less complex than if the objective is a Principle of the model of play (with all its Subprinciples).

Complexity and difficulty impact upon the the team's cognitive load (how hard they have to think about things) at every stage of the process.

For example, you may design a 4v4 drill in which players may only intervene with their less-favored legs, and it will be difficult; or you may design an 8v8 with two neutrals in which the teams are incentivized to press in a high block and such a drill will be an activity of high complexity.

Descriptive factors

- *Rules of engagement.* They are the conditions that allow the coach to build the drill which encourages the appearance of the wanted collective behavior.
- *Space.* The area of play, marked by the movement within the drill and the number of players used.
- *Number of Players.* This includes the players per team as well as the possible neutrals, either defensive or offensive.
- *Time.* Duration, density, number of repetitions, rest between repetitions, number of series, rest between series.

Guided Discovery

Last century, the American educationist, Edgar Dale, established a scale of learning which showed how some methodologies were more effective than others. In it, didactic methods that 'exhibited' information (such as talks, readings, images and videos) were less effective than methods with a more 'constructive' approach like demonstrations, or simulated and direct experiences.

Human beings learn from experience. It is true that is possible to understand, on a theoretical level, a static and one-dimensional reality. However, to internalize complex and dynamic phenomena, it is necessary for the information to come from a personal, direct and repeated experience.

For a team to internalize a model of play, collectively, it is not enough for individual players to just learn a series of movements to perform. It is essential that a player understands the situations that are happening around him, in order to interpret which response is needed for that context and his individual role in that response.

The strongest and longest-lasting individual and collective certainties are built by the players for and by themselves. So, instead of drills (in the traditional sense) *experiences* are proposed. We create tasks where, in a repeated manner, real game situations that demand the development of a certain concept are presented. By directly addressing a certain situation, and with the coach acting as a guide to the process by pointing out the most relevant factors, players will be able to internalize the individual and collective behaviors required by that particular context.

An independent observer is capable of distinguishing, during a game, which team plays with proactive conviction (front foot) and which uses a reactive intuition (back foot play). One way for your team to play with determination requires each player to play with his own personal conviction and share the collective reading of the game with his team.

This is the real spirit that occupies training. Each session is structured within a *morphocycle* (a weekly training regime), which is the overriding structure that sustains the training process. The objective is for the team to arrive in optimal condition on competition day.

The Morphocycle Pattern

The morphocycle pattern is the weekly schedule which gives shape to the structure of training proposed by Tactical Periodization. Its structure will be used from the second week of training to the end of the season. Once we have the model of play dissected into concepts and organized hierarchically in Principles, Subprinciples and Sub-Subprinciples we must take into account the following fundamental methodological features:

Principle of specificity

All the experiences put forward during training must be related to the team's model of play. Players must know the purpose of each drill and maintain a high level of concentration while executing it. Last but not least, the coach must intervene in a timely manner to focus the attention of the team on key aspects – guiding the learning process and helping embed information.

The principle of complex progression

This is related to the hierarchical organization of the principles. Complexity can be added as a player understands and controls elements of the model of play. In other words, start out simple and build up once an element is secured.

The principle of propensities (doing things often)

In essence, this is about designing drills which *repeat* the elements that we want our players to acquire (Principles, Subprinciples, and Sub-Subprinciples).

The principle of horizontal alternation (mixing up the demands you put on your players)

This principle is about regulating the relationship between load and recovery. It requires the coach to vary the type of demand in each session, to ensure optimal recovery. It is not possible for a body to deliver constantly the same effort, every day.

To be able to establish the most suitable format for a morphocycle pattern, we need to establish two more factors:

Number of sessions

In elite football, players perform between five and six weekly training sessions, but for this section (and to keep things simple) we'll assume we have three sessions with our players and one game slot available. One session of passive recovery will also be included.

Number of games per week

Further to the above, since we are not playing European competitions or Cup matches, we'll assume we have a game per week.

So now, with the different conditions noted, we'll dig into the morphocycle.

Session 1: Passive Recovery

After our (weekly) competitive game, and due to the cognitive fatigue that comes with it, we need to release players' minds from the effort made. We do not train. Resting is the 'invisible training' that allows us to compensate against the load.

It is common to see teams 'run out of gas' because coaches have not given them enough recovery from the cognitive load of match days. If players are not allowed to rest, the mental load will build and it will become impossible to train at top intensity during the mid-term, bringing a gradual loss of relative competitiveness in the championship over time.

Session 2: Day of Tension Training

We work the Subprinciples of the game in a complex (game-like) way but always with reduced groups of players, space, and time.

Structure of the session:

Warm-up

Formed by a common block or group of exercises (i.e. general drills) and a block of technical drills within a context (e.g. attacking play with passes behind the defense, but within the context of a 4v5 situation). Between 12 and 20 minutes.

Main block

We divide the group into two subgroups (7 to 10 players each).

Main Block, Drill 1

Tactical tasks that are 3v3, 4v4, 5v5 (with or without neutrals). 1 or 2 series of 5 to 8 repetitions of 3 to 5 minutes. Rests between repetitions of about half of the working time (use the breaks to make the group think about what just happened) and 5 minutes between series. Total volume of work between 10 and 30 minutes.

Main Block, Drill 2

Option 1

High Interval Training. We will perform competitive games of 1v1 and 2v2 (with or without neutrals) of 1 or 2 series of 6 repetitions where you alternate 30/60 seconds of effort and 30/60 seconds of recovery. Total volume of work (taking recovery time into account) of between 6 and 12 minutes.

Option 2

Tactical tasks that are 3v3, 4v4 or 5v5 (with or without neutrals). 1 or 2 series of 4 to 6 repetitions of 1 to 3 minutes. Recovery times between repetitions of the same length as the working time and 3 minutes between series. Total volume of work of between 10 and 20 minutes.

Cool down

Stretching, core exercises, and feedback.

Session 3: Day of Duration Training

Session 3 is the session with the greatest load of the week. The spaces, groups of players, and times will be more testing. Principles and some Subprinciples (experienced unconsciously) will rule the design of the session.

Structure of the session:

Warm-up

Formed by a common block and a block of running technique and coordination.

Between 10 and 15 minutes.

Main Block (whole group)

Tactical tasks that are 8v8, 9v9 (with or without neutrals). 1 or 2 series of 4 to 5 repetitions of 5 to 15 minutes. Rests between repetitions of 1 or 2 minutes (use the breaks to make the group think about what just happened) and 4 minutes between series. Total volume of work of between 30 and 40 minutes.

During the repetitions we can change the rules of the exercise, respecting the same objective of the drill or adding rules that will trigger situations that help to generate collective behaviors in compliance with the values that the coach wants for the group.

Cool down

Stretching and feedback.

Session 4: Day of Speed Training

This session gets closer to the game. Based on Sub-Subprinciples, we will design a session containing drills of low complexity, with little opposition, great decision making, and execution speeds. The load times will be short.

Structure of the session:

Warm-up

Formed by a common block and a block of specific strength actions.

Between 15 and 25 minutes.

Main Block (whole group)

There are two alternatives. A. if the game is in one day, and B. if the game is in two days.

A.   Game in 24H.

Tactical Task 1. Playing 1v1, 2v2, 3v3. One series of five repetitions of 10 seconds of explosive strength with 2 minutes recovery.

Tactical Task 2. One series of three repetitions of three minutes work with two minutes recovery.

Strategic work with possession broken up regularly.

B.   Game in 48H.

Tactical Task 1. Playing 4v4 or 5v5. Two series of four repetitions of 30 seconds with 30 seconds recovery between repetitions and three to five minutes recovery between series. Volume of work between four and 16 minutes.

Tactical Task 2. One series of three repetitions of three minutes work for two minutes recovery.

Strategic work.

Cool down

Feedback and naming the match day team.

The objective is for the players to arrive at their match in the best possible condition. Sometimes it is easy to forget that legs must be fresh, and minds are thinking clearly.

The last session before the game is usually on Friday evening, and the game may be on Saturday, which gives the players less than 24 hours to rest. 24 hours! This is the time to offer very little load (physical and/or cognitive).

Bear in mind that we need to resist the temptation to carry out drills that focus on Principles, or something equivalently complex, on the last day of the morphocycle. Likewise, coaches need to avoid lengthening a drill for pure personal enjoyment or without realising they have done so.

Difficulty versus Complexity

The transmission of the model of play is a thrilling task, and the planning and development of a library of drills is conditioned by several factors.

Depending on how well a team assimilates certain Principles, Subprinciples or Sub-Subprinciples, we increase the difficulty of the exercises. As such, we can establish three levels of difficulty.

The drills must involve a level of complexity that depends on where a team is in the morphocycle pattern, and its current knowledge of the Principles, Subprinciples or Sub-subprinciples. In other words, we maintain the level of difficulty and increase the level of complexity until we climb to the next level of difficulty. For this book, we have established three levels of complexity.

Here is an example of how we could deliver drills that work on the Principle of "Travelling with the ball", the Subprinciple of "Numerical Superiority", and its subsequent Sub-Subprinciples.

E.g.

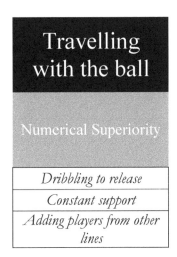

First Stage of Drills

- Drill Name: Numerical Superiority Level 1
- Relating to Principle/Sub-Principle/Sub-Subprinciple: Numerical Superiority and its Sub-Subprinciples: Dribbling to release, Constant support and Adding players from other lines
- Difficulty: Low
- Complexity: 2

[note, the difficulty scale is low-medium-high; complexity is 1-2-3 with 3 being the most complex]

Example drill

Main Objective

Numerical superiority

Teams

4v4

Neutrals

3

Description

Teams are shaped by two central defenders and two midfielders. Neutrals act as wingers and pivots.

Rules of engagement

Each team may defend with only two players in each zone. This way the team in possession feels the advantage of playing with a clear numerical advantage when starting the play, and when progressing to the second zone. They will understand the importance of an offensive temporization, giving time to their teammates to move up the pitch and maintaining numerical superiority.

Second Stage of Drills

- Drill Name: Travelling with the ball Level 1
- Relating to Principle/Sub-Principle/Sub-Subprinciple: Travelling with the ball and its Subprinciple of Numerical Superiority
- Difficulty: Low
- Complexity: 3

Example drill

Main Objective

Travelling with the ball

Teams

6v6

Neutrals

2

Description

Teams are shaped by two central defenders, one pivot, two midfielders and one striker. Neutrals act as wingers.

Rules of Engagement

Each player may only defend their own zone. Each group of players will be assigned a concrete defensive zone. The team in possession will be incentivized to use its numerical superiority in each of the three zones that represent each of the offensive sub-phases. As the team progresses in possession, they might reorder themselves to hold that advantage again and again. That constant use of numerical superiority using the right positioning at every phase is what the Travelling with the Ball Principle is all about.

Third Stage of Drills

- Drill Name: Dribbling to release Level 1
- Relating to Principle/Sub-Principle/Sub-Subprinciple: Dribbling to release
- Difficulty: Medium
- Complexity: 1

- Drill Name: Constant Support Level 1
- Relating to Principle/Sub-Principle/Sub-Subprinciple: Constant Support
- Difficulty: Medium
- Complexity: 1

- Drill Name: Adding players from other lines Level 1
- Relating to Principle/Sub-Principle/Sub-Subprinciple: Adding players from other lines
- Difficulty: Medium
- Complexity: 1

Example drill

Main Objective

Dribbling to release

Teams

5v5

Neutrals

1

Description

Teams are shaped by two central defenders, two midfielders, and one striker. The neutrals act as pivots.

Rules of Engagement

The ball may not be stolen from the ball holder unless he is motionless or if he has already made three touches on the ball. Pass interception is allowed, though. This way, ball holders will be incentivized to drive the ball using their three first touches to create clear passing lines. That short drive with the ball is the key to freeing passing lines. Additionally, teammates will be patient, holding their positions (positional game), allowing the ball holder to find the pass.

Example drill

Main Objective

Constant support

Teams

2v2v2

Neutrals

0

Description

Two teams in possession and one team trying to get the ball.

Rules of Engagement

Players may move sideways to support the ball holder and create passing lines. Once the team on the inside gets the ball, they pass it to the other team in possession and position themselves accordingly to receive the ball back. The team that loses the ball tries to press instantly to stop the first pass.

Example drill

Main Objective

Adding players from other lines

Teams

2v2v2

Neutrals

1

Description

"Rondo" Game. Two teams in possession and one team trying to get the ball. One neutral in a central position.

Rules of Engagement

Players may move sideways to support the ball holder and create passing lines. If the ball moves to the next square, players in possession have to move to support the ball in the opposite square. Once the team on the inside gets the ball, they pass it to the other team in possession and position themselves accordingly to receive the ball back.

Fourth Stage of Drills

- Drill Name: Numerical Superiority Level 2
- Relating to Principle/Sub-Principle/Sub-Subprinciple: Numerical Superiority and its Sub-Subprinciples: Dribbling to release, Constant support and Adding players from other lines
- Difficulty: Medium
- Complexity: 2

Example drill

Main Objective

Numerical superiority

Teams

5v5 plus goalkeepers

Neutrals

2

Description

Teams are shaped by two central defenders, one pivot, and two midfielders. Neutrals act as wingers.

Rules of Engagement

Each team may defend with a maximum of three players in each zone. This way the team in possession witnesses the advantage of playing with a clear numerical advantage when starting the play and when progressing to the second. When accessing a new zone, where the importance of an offensive temporization is clear, giving time for teammates to move up the pitch and maintain numerical superiority is key. In this drill, one of the defending players may return to the first zone to increase difficulty.

Fifth Stage of Drills

- Drill Name: Travelling with the ball Level 2
- Relating to Principle/Sub-Principle/Sub-Subprinciple: Travelling with the ball and its Subprinciple Numerical Superiority
- Difficulty: Medium
- Complexity: 3

Example drill

Main Objective

Travelling with the ball

Teams

7v7 plus goalkeepers

Neutrals

0

Description

Teams are shaped by three defenders, one pivot, two midfielders and one striker.

Rules of Engagement

Each player may only defend their own zone. Each group of players will be assigned a concrete defensive zone. The team in possession will be incentivized to use its numerical superiority in each of the three zones that represent each of the offensive sub-phases. As the team progresses, whilst in possession, they might reorder themselves to gain advantage again and again. The constant use of numerical superiority, using the right positioning at every phase, is what the Travelling with the ball Principle is all about.

This drill is more difficult than the Level 1 version because of the number of players defending the last zone; it will demand a better interpretation of offensive order when arriving at the finishing zone(s).

Sixth Stage of Drills

- Drill Name: Dribbling to release Level 2
- Relating to Principle/Sub-Principle/Sub-Subprinciple: Dribbling to release
- Difficulty: High
- Complexity: 1

- Drill Name: Constant Support Level 2
- Relating to Principle/Sub-Principle/Sub-Subprinciple: Constant Support
- Difficulty: High
- Complexity: 1

- Drill Name: Adding players from other lines Level 2
- Relating to Principle/Sub-Principle/Sub-Subprinciple: Adding players from other lines
- Difficulty: High
- Complexity: 1

Example drill

Main Objective

Dribbling to release

Teams

5v5

Neutrals

0

Description

Teams are shaped in a 1-1-2-1 formation

Rules of Engagement

Each player may only defend their own zone. When attacking, they may only operate in their own zone except when passing from one zone to the next by driving the ball. They score a point when they successfully drive the ball to the last line. During the drill, players will soon come to understand that the best way to progress with the ball is by driving it from one zone to the next. In turn, a player will be able to free his teammate and allow him to pass the ball safely. That free man will drive the ball to the next zone to accomplish the same objective.

Example drill

Main Objective

Constant support

Teams

3v3v3

Neutrals

0

Description

"Rondo" Game. Two teams in possession and one team trying to get the ball. The two teams in possession shape up as follows. Teams: left centre back, left inside midfielder and right midfielder; Neutrals: full backs and pivot.

Rules of Engagement

Players may move to support the ball holder and create passing lines. They are constantly shaping a small square next to the ball whilst occupying the big square too. So it is best to place four players in the big square and two players to complete the small one. This constant repositioning will simulate the constant support needed during the game. Once the team inside gets the ball, they pass it to the neutrals that are still in possession and position themselves accordingly.

Example drill

Main Objective

Adding players from other lines

Teams

3v3

Neutrals

0

Description

Two teams shaped in a 1-2-1 formation.

Rules of Engagement

Each player may only defend their own zone. Finishing is only allowed from the second zone. This drill will force players who are sitting in the defensive zone to move up to get a finishing position (starting from a position of numerical inferiority). The team in possession will have to be risk-averse in their ball possession; as the defenders come up, they must finish on goal in order not to concede counter attacks.

Seventh Stage of Drills

- Drill Name: Numerical Superiority Level 3
- Relating to Principle/Sub-Principle/Sub-Subprinciple: Numerical Superiority and its Sub-Subprinciples
- Difficulty: High
- Complexity: 2

Example drill

Main Objective

Numerical superiority

Teams

5v5

Neutrals

0

Description

In possession, teams are shaped by two central defenders, one pivot, and two midfielders. When out of possession, teams are shaped by two central defenders, two midfielders, and one striker.

Rules of Engagement

Each team may defend with a maximum of two players in each zone. The same conditions and total space are in place as per the Level 2 drill of the same content. There are two differences to increase difficulty: 1) the absence of neutrals and 2) the three zones that force the team in possession to face an opposing team with defensive depth.

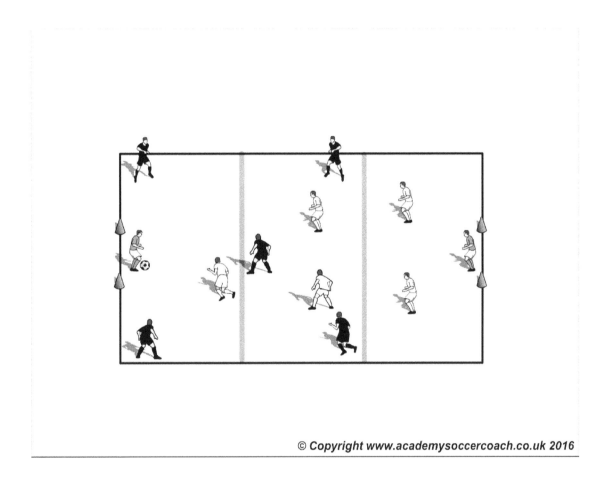

Eighth Stage of Drills

- Drill Name: Travelling with the ball Level 3
- Relating to Principle/Sub-Principle/Sub-Subprinciple: Travelling with the ball and its Subprinciple Numerical Superiority
- Difficulty: High
- Complexity: 3

Example drill

Main Objective

Travelling with the ball

Teams

7v7

Neutrals

0

Description

Teams are shaped by three defenders, one pivot, two midfielders, and one striker.

Rules of Engagement

Each player may only defend their own zone. When in possession, a player has unlimited touches in his zone and only one touch outside it. There is one exception: when a player in possession drives the ball from his zone to the next one (in this case, and during that play, he will have unlimited touches there too).

The difference between this drill and stage five's is the conditioning of the behavior of players in possession. In stage five, they are allowed to attack freely. In this one, their touches may be limited depending on where they are and how they got there.

Planning

Now that we have clarified the model of play through Principles, Subprinciples, and Sub-Subprinciples, and learnt about the morphocycle, we are ready to plan some more. In the first part, we shall shed light on which concepts to work on, and how to link them. In the second part, we shall examine which tasks to undertake depending on the day of the week. Our planning will tell us when to introduce tasks related to a certain concept and what level of difficulty to provide. During the planning process we must take the following factors into account:

1. The set of interrelated Principles, Subprinciples, and Sub-Subprinciples that will shape our play.
2. The morphocycle, understood as the structure and weekly unit of training that establishes the conditions under which we run exercises.
3. The learned state/progress of each model of play element. Friendlies, and competitive games are the real test for evaluating whether the tactical concepts that shape the model of game have been acquired by the players. After each competitive encounter, the coach may reconsider coaching priorities for the week ahead.

Before beginning match day training (e.g. in-season training), it is necessary to plan six weeks of preseason and make sure that, over those 18 active sessions, we have covered all the concepts underpinning our model of play so that we hit the ground running in week 1 of competition.

The Preseason

The first week of preseason is all about adapting to the specific load of football practice, so it is important that the cognitive load (how hard players have to think) is not excessive (we're all getting our heads straight after time off on holiday). It is a week during which we focus on the volume of work rather than complexity. We will introduce drills that focus on Sub-Subprinciples during the second week.

From the second week onwards, we structure the training week in exactly the same way as we plan to train our players right up to the end of the season. On the first day of the week, we will cover Subprinciples, the second day Principles, and the third Sub-Subprinciples.

If our model of play dictates…

1. Travelling together with the ball, with numerical superiority, during the offensive moment.
2. A pressing retreat, with zonal marking, during the defensive moment.

… then it is desirable that in each training session we cover two (no more than three) tactical concepts (besides the technical and psychological ones) to bring about this model of play.

Pedagogic Planning of the Offensive Moment

	PRESEASON																	
	Week 1			Week 2			Week 3			Week 4			Week 5			Week 6		
Day of the Week →	1	2	3	1	2	3	1	2	3	1	2	3	1	2	3	1	2	3

MOMENT	LEVEL	CONTENT	1	2	3	1	2	3	1	2	3	1	2	3	1	2	3	1	2	3
Positional Attack	Principle	Travelling with the ball					1												2	
Positional Attack	SubPrinciple	Numerical Superiority				1												1		
Positional Attack	SubSubPrinciple	Dribbling to release			1															
Positional Attack	SubSubPrinciple	Constant support	1																	
Positional Attack	SubSubPrinciple	Adding players from other lines	1																	
Positional Attack	SubPrinciple	Rational Occupation of Space																1		
Positional Attack	SubSubPrinciple	Relational Distances			1												1			
Positional Attack	SubSubPrinciple	Receivers at different lengths of pass															1			
Positional Attack	SubSubPrinciple	Width															1			
Positional Attack	SubSubPrinciple	Depth															1			
Positional Attack	SubSubPrinciple	Securing possession zone																		
Positional Attack	SubPrinciple	Pace of Play																		
Positional Attack	SubPrinciple	Patience and Continuity																		
Positional Attack	SubSubPrinciple	Offensive Temporizations																		
Positional Attack	SubSubPrinciple	Support behind the line of the ball																		
Positional Attack	Principle	Creating Space					1													
Positional Attack	SubPrinciple	Finding the free man				1														
Positional Attack	SubSubPrinciple	Dribbling to Release		1																
Positional Attack	SubSubPrinciple	Pace of play with near players		1																
Positional Attack	SubSubPrinciple	Attract to free up further players		1																
Positional Attack	SubPrinciple	Width and Depth																		
Positional Attack	SubPrinciple	Interchange of Positions																		
Positional Attack	SubSubPrinciple	Incoporation of first line players																		
Positional Attack	SubSubPrinciple	Movements to break in the second line																		
Positional Attack	SubSubPrinciple	Movements to break in the third line																		
Positional Attack	SubPrinciple	Third Man																		

* The number in each column refers to the difficulty of the session, 1 being easiest.

If a cell has no number in it, it is not being trained at that time.

The attacking elements of our model of play (which are worked during preseason) are the ones that will provide our team's identity.

Pedagogic Planning of the Defensive Moment

MOMENT	LEVEL	CONTENT	Week 1 1	Week 1 2	Week 1 3	Week 2 1	Week 2 2	Week 2 3	Week 3 1	Week 3 2	Week 3 3	Week 4 1	Week 4 2	Week 4 3	Week 5 1	Week 5 2	Week 5 3	Week 6 1	Week 6 2	Week 6 3
Pressing Defense	Principle	Retreat								1						2			2	
Pressing Defense	SubPrinciple	Zonal Marking							1											
Pressing Defense	SubSubPrinciple	Hounding opposition with the ball						1												
Pressing Defense	SubSubPrinciple	Vigilance without the Ball						1												
Pressing Defense	SubSubPrinciple	Covering nearby zones						1												
Pressing Defense	SubPrinciple	Defending higher up													1					
Pressing Defense	SubSubPrinciple	Defensive timing. Avoiding Advance												1						
Pressing Defense	SubSubPrinciple	Advance in pass backs and turned opposition												1						
Pressing Defense	SubSubPrinciple	Watching our backs and sideways												1						
Pressing Defense	SubPrinciple	Press and Screen																		
Pressing Defense	SubSubPrinciple	Screening lines of pass																		
Pressing Defense	SubSubPrinciple	Hounding the ball carrier																		
Pressing Defense	SubPrinciple	Defensive depth																1		
Pressing Defense	SubSubPrinciple	Reducing space in depth														1				
Pressing Defense	SubSubPrinciple	Reducing space in width														1				
Pressing Defense	SubSubPrinciple	Defensive stepping														1				
Pressing Defense	Principle	Pressure								1										
Pressing Defense	SubPrinciple	Press and screen							1											
Pressing Defense	SubSubPrinciple	Set marks						1												
Pressing Defense	SubSubPrinciple	Screening lines of pass						1												
Pressing Defense	SubSubPrinciple	Generating defensive superiority						1												
Pressing Defense	SubPrinciple	Gain height																		
Pressing Defense	SubSubPrinciple	Vigilance																		
Pressing Defense	SubSubPrinciple	Push the line																		
Pressing Defense	SubSubPrinciple	Relative distance																		

The defensive moment will be the moment most worked during preseason. It is the one that will give our team the consistency and the capacity to compete.

Pedagogic Planning of Transitions

			PRESEASON																		
			Week 1			Week 2			Week 3			Week 4			Week 5			Week 6		
	Day of the Week →		1	2	3	1	2	3	1	2	3	1	2	3	1	2	3	1	2	3
MOMENT	**LEVEL**	**CONTENT**																		
Defensive transition	Principle	Pressure vs retreat										1								
Defensive Transition	Subprinciple	Pressure: defensive numerical superiority										1								
Defensive Transition	Subprinciple	Pressing retreat										1								
Defensive Transition	Subprinciple	Selecting the defensive height										1								
Offensive Transition	Principle	Using free spaces vs temporization																		
Offensive Transition	Subprinciple	Using free spaces																		
Offensive Transition	Subprinciple	Offensive temporization																		

During these transitional exercises in pre-season, defensive transitions have priority since they are key to the behavior of the team. It is imperative to link transitions, overall, to a team's attacking and defensive capabilities – as soon as possible – to give coherence to the model.

Pedagogic Planning of the Model of Play in Set Pieces

			PRESEASON					
Day of the Week →			Week 1 1 2 3	Week 2 1 2 3	Week 3 1 2 3	Week 4 1 2 3	Week 5 1 2 3	Week 6 1 2 3
MOMENT LEVEL		**CONTENT**						
Strategy								
Defensive Strategy	SubSubPrinciple	Corners			1	2	3	4
Defensive Strategy	SubSubPrinciple	Goal kicks	1		2			
Defensive Strategy	SubSubPrinciple	Free kicks						
Defensive Strategy	SubSubPrinciple	Throws			1	2		3
Defensive Strategy	SubSubPrinciple	Kick offs						
Offensive Strategy	SubSubPrinciple	Corners						
Offensive Strategy	SubSubPrinciple	Goal kicks	1		2			3
Offensive Strategy	SubSubPrinciple	Free kicks		1				
Offensive Strategy	SubSubPrinciple	Throws			1	2		3
Offensive Strategy	SubSubPrinciple	Kick offs						

The polishing of the technical and tactical actions of our 'play' must be planned in relation to the rest of the preseason's training plan.

MOMENT	LEVEL	CONTENT	Week 1 1	Week 1 2	Week 1 3	Week 2 1	Week 2 2	Week 2 3	Week 3 1	Week 3 2	Week 3 3	Week 4 1	Week 4 2	Week 4 3	Week 5 1	Week 5 2	Week 5 3	Week 6 1	Week 6 2	Week 6 3
Contextualized technique																				
Technical Actions	Ways of	Recuperating the ball																1		
Technical Actions	Ways of	Relation through Pass	1			1														
Technical Actions	Ways of	Shots on goal																		
Technical Actions	Ways of	Headers																1		
Set Piece Technique	Ways of	Throw ins							1											
Set Piece Technique	Ways of	Crosses																		
Set Piece Technique	Ways of	Regain possession						1				1								
Set Piece Technique	Ways of	Guess movements													1					

Day of the Week →

Pedagogic Planning of Contextualised Technique

The polishing of technical/tactical "play" must be planned in relation to all other preseason content.

			PRESEASON																		
			Week 1			Week 2			Week 3			Week 4			Week 5			Week 6		
Day of the Week →			1	2	3	1	2	3	1	2	3	1	2	3	1	2	3	1	2	3
MOMENT LEVEL		**CONTENT**																			
Contextualised technique																					
Technical Actions	Ways of	Recovering the ball																1		
Technical Actions	Ways of	Communicating through passing	1			1														
Technical Actions	Ways of	Shots on goal																		
Technical Actions	Ways of	Headers																1		
Set Piece Technique	Ways of	Throw ins							1											
Set Piece Technique	Ways of	Crosses																		
Set Piece Technique	Ways of	Regaining possession						1				1								
Set Piece Technique	Ways of	Anticipating movements													1					

74

Pedagogic Planning of Psychological Values

Putting any 'collective way of playing' into practice demands players to experience certain shared values, and the coach must cement these values in training and whenever the group is together. On duration days, introduce drills that help develop these values as they progress.

			PRESEASON					
			Week 1	Week 2	Week 3	Week 4	Week 5	Week 6
Day of the Week →			1 2 3	1 2 3	1 2 3	1 2 3	1 2 3	1 2 3

MOMENT LEVEL		CONTENT	Week 1	Week 2	Week 3	Week 4	Week 5	Week 6
Identity								
Values	Collective	Ambition						
Values	Collective	Cooperation				1		
Values	Collective	Aggression			1			
Values	Collective	Dedication						
Values	Collective	Communication		1				2
Values	Collective	Concentration	1				2	
Values	Collective	Security						

Common Questions

Do we have to deal with all 'model of play' concepts before the season starts?

No, we do not. Working on too many concepts can harm our players' acquisition of the model of play and bring about stress that will diminish their confidence. Focus on the most important concepts.

This planning all looks very abstract. When do we work on playing from the back or defending crosses?

Build up, creative play, and finishing are not game moments in themselves. We will address them when we apply the Principles (plus Subprinciples and Sub-Subprinciples) to those phases of the game. For example, we will carry out a drill of "constant support" with regard to build up play and (afterwards) – in a drill of "numerical superiority" – we will see how that concept is specifically applied.

Periodizing Technique

Tactical Periodization is a methodology that develops fitness training and technique as a *consequence* of the approach. A systemic vision of the sport makes little sense, by comparison, and the idea of separating the training of different skills for developing footballing excellence likewise. Thus, technical skills and physical skills are developed through tactical training. Real improvements can be gained!

It was not until I heard Marcelo Bielsa talking about the technical dimension that I started to realize the true value of complementing tactical work with technical tasks.

Once upon a time, Marcelo Bielsa, after a defeat, got ready to watch the video of the game. He did so to calm his conscience and find ways to improve. On this occasion, his analysis moved away from player attitude or tactical deficiencies, and he noticed that his players had failed a series of different defensive technical actions, which separated them from victory that night.

Bielsa realised that his players failed to utilise the appropriate actions due to an ignorance of which action was appropriate at that moment or because they lacked the confidence to deploy that action. Marcelo decided, after that, that his players would experience every type of technical action in the game; within the context of any match they could 1) choose the most effective action 2) execute it with the confidence of someone who knows what they are doing.

I would like to clarify that I am not advocating the introduction of traditional technical drills. Neither am I talking about ousting the tactical supradimension for the technical. Rather, I am looking to reinforce the cognitive dimension of the game by experiencing and developing technical actions appropriate to particular contexts. In other words, we do not want to just improve technical skills (they will improve as a consequence of our training) we want to help the player to recognize the movement of the game – as a whole – so that his decision making becomes more effective.

How should we work on technique?

There are a great number of different technical actions. Different types of shot, different ways to dribble, different ways to steal the ball from the opposition, different ways to control a pass or make one, different ways to extinguish pressure, to cross a ball or to screen it.

And of these techniques, some will be more appropriate than others depending on the context of the game at the time. For instance, when controlling a strong pass that comes from the line behind (for example, from defence into midfield), it will be more effective to control the ball with the furthest leg so that our body orientation helps us make progress with the ball. If the pass is not that strong, it might be better to use the closest leg to shield the ball from an attempted tackle. So, in a sense, our aim is to train players so that:

1. The player feels comfortable performing a technical action in a contextualized situation (and with opposition).
2. The player is able to choose, consciously first *and subconsciously in due course*, which action is most appropriate for each situation and his skillset.

In summary, training tasks will have a main technical objective in contextualized situations, and we work to develop decision-making that later on should be supported in open tactical tasks.

Is this approach compatible with Tactical Periodization?

Strictly speaking, this approach is not compatible with TP as professor Frade defines it. However, there is a place in our particular morphocycle. It is about reproducing fragments of the game that allow the player to respond with greater efficiency, and in full command of the Principles of our play. We can call it contextualized technique or decision-making training.

Next, we examine all the technical actions, broken up, depending on the contextual variables that we consider most relevant.

Headers

Depending on movement

- Attacking the ball
- Running backwards
- Anticipating position(s)
- Static and fighting for position

Depending on the contact surface of the head

- Frontal
- Flick-on
- Turning the head to one side
- Turning the head to the other side

Depending on intention

- Elevate
- Head the ball to the ground
- Power

Depending on the trajectory of the ball

- Frontal
- Diagonal-Frontal
- Cross at the same height

Kicks on goal

Depending on movement

- First touch shot
- After dribbling to the outside
- After dribbling to the inside
- After a 360° turn
- After a one-on-one with the keeper

Depending on the trajectory of the pass

- Side pass backwards
- Side pass forwards
- Frontal pass
- Free ball
- Deflected ball

Depending on the type of pass

- Lob
- Flat
- Bouncing

Depending on the target

- Near post
- Far post
- Lob

Combination play through the pass

Body Position of the receiver (and implications for the receiver)

- Back to goal (the receiver must pass the ball back along the line it came from)
- Sideways (depending on the controlling leg, the receiver can choose to progress or pass the ball back along the line it came).
- Facing goal (the receiver must search for a free man in his line (or a higher one) in order to advance; otherwise, he will have to pass the ball backwards. Passing backwards should be a last resort and only carried out if there is no possibility of continuing with the advance).

Receiving leg

- Leg closer to goal (will force the receiver to pass the ball back along the line it came from).
- Leg away from goal (the receiver must search for a free man in his line (or a higher one) in order to advance; otherwise, he will have to pass the ball backwards. Passing backwards should be a last resort and only carried out if there is no possibility of continuing with the advance).

Position of the pass

- Pass to feet (the receiver will have to assess where the advantage can be gained. If he has it, he should try to dribble. Failing that, he must hold the ball or if a teammate is available must pass the ball to him fast).

- Pass to space (choices here include whether to finish, to dribble, or move the ball to another player already in an advantageous position).

Throw-ins

Throw in to get the ball back and create a 2 on 1 against the defender

Long throw for a flick on

- Inside the box
- Outside the box
- Short frontal or diagonal throw-ins to carry on with play

Robbing the ball

From behind

- Anticipation
- Movement (before a pass is made, the receiver must take up his position or move away from the line of the ball to draw the defender)
- Slide tackle

From the side

- Charge
- Tackle

From the front

- Blocking

Running

- Winning the position

The role of keep ups and other related ability challenges

Keep ups and skill games relate to the operation of particular technical skills. I am not referring to individual simple keep ups (i.e. juggling a ball foot-to-foot as an individual) but to a collective ability to keep a ball off the ground where players collaborate to achieve a particular goal.

In itself, this technical skill might appear to offer little benefit to the game. However, keep up-based drills require superior ability and can prove highly beneficial in reinforcing the socio-emotional structure of the team, the collaborative spirit amongst teammates, and self-confidence in individuals.

Practice will bring about increases in a player's technical self-esteem and ball control confidence. Pep Guardiola´s rondos may have been a popular public face of Barcelona's training, but collective keep up games (although less public) were present in day-to-day practice. Soon after Guardiola's arrival at Manchester City, videos of the squad completing these keep up exercises began to surface.

Planning and Training the Model of Play: Set Pieces

Set pieces are, by their very nature, different to the flowing, organic and chaotic activity that comes with open play. But set pieces also adhere to the model of play. It is no longer about a number of movements offered by the coach and practiced once a week. It is about being able to put into action your game model no matter how the game is resumed.

Every element of the model of play requires the team to master it and 'feel' it as its own. The model of play incorporates the simplest tactical concept right through to the most complex one. This means that training must follow the Principle of Complex Progression and the Principle of Propensities. To remind you:

- **The Principle of Complex Progression.** Prioritize your playing Principles. Choose which are most important. Increase complexity as the players' understanding grows and as they master the concepts underlying your model of play.
- **The Principle of Propensities.** Create training exercises so that players experience as much of a Principle, SubPrinciple or Sub-Subprinciple as possible during your sessions. For example, you would not train a micro concept like near post shooting through an 11v11 game on a full-size pitch.

We cannot ignore that when we carefully choreograph players' movements (e.g. at set pieces), their involvement diminishes, their attention reduces and feelings of ownership dissipate. With these (potentially) negative factors swirling around, we must be very clear how we want to attack and defend set pieces. And when I say "how" I do not mean which movements to make but which ones to provoke.

This document states that the principles that guide offensive set pieces must be the same as for the offensive moment (i.e. open play) of the team, so the message soaks in more consistently:

- Generating Numerical Superiority. (Dominant Subprinciple in Travelling Together)
- Finding the Free Man. (Dominant Subprinciple in the Principle of Generating Spaces).

The principles that will guide the defense of set pieces will also be coherent for the defensive moments of the team:

80

- Pressure in a high block whenever possible.
- Full pitch pressing, zonal marking on retreat as an alternative. For defensive actions that deal with a cross, we will have to take into account two key aspects of zonal marking: blocking runs alongside anticipating positions where a finish is viable; and holding positional advantage.

Type of actions

It is essential to prepare the team to defend and attack each and all of the actions listed next. They are all important and mastering each of them will allow the team to get closer to game domination.

1. Goal kick
2. Throw in
3. Corner and close free kick
4. Far free kick
5. Kick off

It is crucial to have a clear application of the principles of the model of play for each of these actions; patterns of attack and defense must be established for each of them. During training, the coach should be able to focus on training each of these restart scenarios (from goal kicks to kick offs).

Training Set Pieces

It is important to prepare and train defensive actions first. This way, our players will learn from real experience all about offensive behaviors at set pieces. We will then apply those defensive concepts to the way we attack similar set pieces. We must schedule the exercises for training the model of play; it can be that one day we do phases 1 and 2 and two weeks after, on another day of the week, we do phase 3. That is to say that the following phases (below) do not have to be done together in the same session. They can be planned in a discontinuous way and all the phases can be worked into any sessions of the week.

Phase 0

Before working on each set piece, the team must know sufficiently the fundamentals of the Principle or Subprinciple that will guide the process of the specific action. Additionally, it is optimal that before the training of the action we perform some contextualized technical work which is relevant to that set piece. For instance, if you are going to train how to defend long punts from goal kicks it might be really useful to have players estimating ball trajectories (and heading balls) during warm up.

Phase 1

Explanation on a blackboard, presenting an overview of the situation; what we are intending to do, and what advantages we will gain in doing so.

Phase 2

This Phase will differ depending on whether we are working on set piece attack or defence:

- For attack, we will design rondos (or any other possession games) where the restart (understanding it as the *beginning* of the set piece) will be performed every time we resume the drill. In other words, a set piece such as a throw in will initiate the possession game, and any time the ball goes dead, another throw in will recommence proceedings.
- For defence, we will design small-sided games of 2v2 where we continuously repeat the action we want to learn. For instance, when practicing how to defend a direct throw-in to the box, a 2v2 small-sided game will be presented in which all throw-ins must be placed into the box; and every time the game restarts it does so via a throw-in.

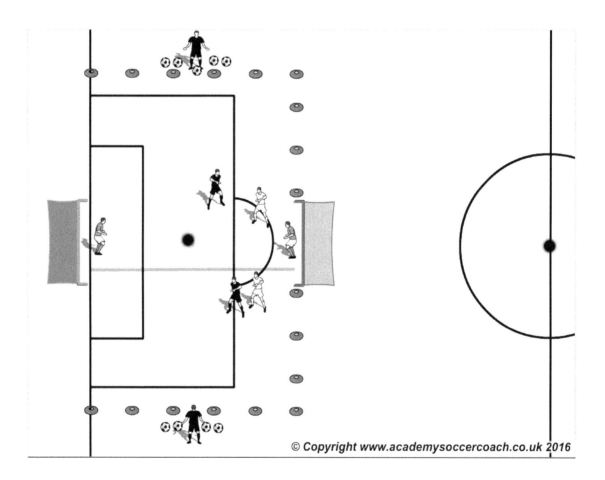

© Copyright www.academysoccercoach.co.uk 2016

Phase 3

Small-sided games of 3v3 or 4v4 where we continuously repeat the action we want to work on, and establish the behaviours we want to strengthen.

Phase 4

This Phase is exclusive to the training of offensive set pieces. We will generate situations close to the real game with limited opposition. The game will restart from the chosen situation again and again.

Phase 5

Small-sided games of 7v7 or 8v8 where the games are restarted every time from the set piece we are working on. We will establish rules to strengthen the behaviors we want to encourage. For instance, if we are defending an action (a throw in, free kick, goal kick or corner kick) through zonal marking we use cones to help players visualize each player's zone of responsibility.

Phase 6

This Phase is exclusive to the training of defensive set pieces. We will generate situations close to the real game where attackers hold a numerical superiority. The game will restart from the chosen situation again and again.

Reinforcing the feeling of responsibility

A coach wants a team to feel responsible for its actions, and we also want them to feel the psychological sensation of being focused. In turn, it is a good idea to have a recorded metric to follow up performances. One easy way to achieve this is to count the number of goals scored and the number of goals prevented. Keep the numbers up-to-date and show them to the team weekly.

Key factors in the success of offensive and defensive strategies

For the coach to evaluate the success of his or her training, with regard to set pieces, he or she should think about the following success factors:

Execution and shooting technique

Feeling good. If practice has been successful, a coach should actually feel pleased (subjective, yes, but a powerful indicator), once things have come to an end, by his team's execution of the technical actions required.

Base physical and psychological conditions

Successfully identifying the strength, height, speed, aggression or courage needed to perform well for the specific set piece. Some of these characteristics may be estimated through training to a certain extent. However, it is crucial to design set piece plays that correspond to our team's characteristics.

Knowledge (and mastery) of situations and contexts

A complete process of training is needed to allow for intense, precise and intelligent matchday execution. The coach may, of course, provide some advice in real time during a game but real success comes from on-pitch autonomy by the team. Until the team feels properly comfortable with the way they interpret set pieces – more practice is needed.

Feeling of responsibility

When each player fully understands their function in the model of play (during every set piece) – can the team maximise performance? This means that the players take responsibility for executing set play strategies at each of the more than 100 set pieces that take place during a single game.

Concluding Remarks

Understanding and learning about a complex system (in this case a group of players) is a living process. Therefore, it is unthinkable that the session-by-session planning explained in this document stops once preseason ends. The process of analyzing and helping players acquire the model of play (and then feeding back into sessions and tasks) is a continuous process, influenced day-by-day and during competition.

It is not unlikely that the six weeks we have planned will not go quite as anticipated or expected. There will inevitably be modifications to content and ways of coaching.

Also, once a team has passed through preseason and into the season proper, it will be the analysis of the team's model of play status, together with the challenges brought by specific opponents, that will guide the training and coaching methods used each week. Always remember to respect the morphocycle.

Acquisition Indicators

The subjective observation of the game by coaching staff is a key aspect to both player and team development. The staff are the ones responsible for observing the presence and interaction of the many variables of the model of play in all their complexity. In turn, it is desirable that several indicators define how the team is progressing in its acquisition of the model of play. These indicators should be judged and recorded during every single game – from the first day of the preseason to the last day of competition.

In this section, I'll put forward three basic indicators; indicators which are very easy to count. They are capable of measuring the state of acquisition of a high number of aspects of the model of play:

  1. Number of times that a team has reached the final third of the opposition's

territory, with the ball in possession, with some spacio-temporal advantage.

2. Number of finishing opportunities.
3. Number of times that the *opposing* team has had possession with spacio-temporal advantage in our half.

The first indicator will demonstrate whether our possession is of high enough quality in areas where we can really hurt the opposition. If we do not have possession here, it likely means that we are losing the ball in the initiation phases of play and we are not capable of generating space in the creative subphase.

The second indicator is a reflection of positional attack. If our attacks die near the edge of the box (and we do not get a chance to finish), it shows that we are not working the space and the opposition well enough. All of the tactical principles that guide the attacking phase aim to create spacio-temporal advantages in finishing areas to increase goal scoring effectiveness. If we are not seeing finishing opportunities, it may mean that we are not succeeding in putting our model of play into action.

The third indicator will tell us if we are pressing high enough up the pitch. We should be subduing and disorganizing the opposition after losing the ball in their half if we want to be successful.

These indicators are not just significant on their own but also flag up related information:

1. Possession in the final third is an indicator of whether the team is travelling together or not.
2. The number of finishing opportunities in relation to the amount of possession with spacio-temporal advantages is a very clear indicator of whether the team knows *how* to generate space in the finishing zone.

The three listed indicators are easy to gather and help to compare the progress of a team between games. They also help to gauge the evolution of the acquisition of the model of play during the season. Sometimes we may have to turn to them to answer the question: What is happening? Are we playing well with regards to our model of play? What content should we train this week?

Reducing the chances of suffering counterattacks

Let's envisage our team at play.

We are taking the initiative. We are stringing together passes in each zone and travelling together. We are accumulating advantages in the final third of the pitch. We allow passing lines to progress with the play, and the more passes we

85

play the deeper the opposition is forced back with more and more players camping out behind the ball. Space gets squeezed in the final quarter of the pitch.

We are working well, and getting close to the opposition's goal. However, the number of opposing players between us and the goal makes it difficult to finish plays with precision. We shoot from mid-distance but luck is not on our side and we do not look like scoring. Play from the outside areas of the pitch is proving unsuccessful because the center is always packed with defenders, and our attackers find themselves at a numerical and positional disadvantage.

We are playing well, moving the ball at a good speed and all the spacio-temporal advantages are in place, until we crash against the defensive wall. And then… tragedy!

One bad interaction with the ball between our midfielders is all it takes. The ball is robbed, the opposition attack, and we are a goal down.

From that moment there are two options:

1. You curse your bad luck, the luck that saw the opposition take their only goal-scoring chance. You curse the slow speed of the defenders or the poor positioning of the goalkeeper. Cursing avoids responsibility.
2. You understand that the defensive phase begins when you are on offense. You understand that a team not only suffers from a counterattack but that the team also caused it to happen.

I have identified two ways to attack (within this model of play) that makes the defensive transition impossible if the opposing team utilises direct play.

1. If we orientate the game to a zone where we do not have numerical superiority, and there is a chance of losing the ball, we are doomed. It will be impossible to press or to retreat effectively through the defensive temporization because we are outgunned.
2. When a team is circulating the ball, there is a big temptation to progress through the inside corridor. When a defending team retreats, they tend to prioritize their defensive efforts on the central zone. This frequently results in lost passes between the center back and midfielder or a horizontal pass between inside players. Against retreated teams, when you want to pass from the building up zone to the goal creating one, it is convenient to find the progression on the outside where there is more advantage and the loss is less dangerous.

Ways to relieve the headaches caused by counter attacks

There are ways to avoid the carnage of counter attacks. I will group them in two:

1.   Variations of the system or players' positions.
1.1.   Playing with three center backs is a good "airbag". It allows the center

backs to advance and press to dispossess the opposition and can offer more coverage against opposing attackers that get free of their markers during transition.

1.2. Playing with a double pivot. In this way, you are more likely to have support behind the ball in all zones of the field, mitigating pressure after losing the ball.

1.3. Positioning one of the full backs on the inside when you are attacking. You form a double pivot with the winger on the other side. This way, you obtain the advantages of 1.2 without modifying the system.

2. Demanding a better interpretation of how the game is played. This results in increased cognitive load on the players.

For this second point, you will need a squad with enough tactical understanding to see what is unfolding in front of them. They must execute (without hesitation) the positional game plan, understanding that it is important to appreciate the value of safety (minimizing risks) during the game. In turn, the team will be able (once explained and trained) to circulate the ball in zones of superiority, and understand that you progress on the outside to finish it inside. They will also understand how crucial it is to constantly provide support behind the ball in order to offer continuity in possession, and to press efficiently after losing the ball.

Without a doubt, the last one (2. Demanding a better interpretation of how the game is played) is the ideal solution, but also the most demanding one. It needs talent from the players and perseverance from the coach.

Conclusion

This book tries to provide a theoretical base and a practical push for any team to develop the 'play' that the Barça of Guardiola developed during his second season. The six weeks of preseason are the beginning of the learning process, because after that period, the team still has a long way to go.

The collective learning for this model of play is complex and requires more time and energy than more common models of play. If a club, or a coach, decides to develop this way of playing, everyone must be aware of its implications over the short, medium and long-term and the maturation time required.

In this book, I express my conviction that this model of play is one of the most competitive ones when it has reached a good level of development; it can elevate the capacities of its players to fully exploit their knowledge of the game, and it makes the team less dependent on individuals. I do not think it was a coincidence that the Spanish national team (with its core of players from the Barça of Guardiola) won the World Cup of 2010, or that the German national team (with its core of players from the Bayern of Guardiola) won the World Cup of 2014.

I believe it is time to go back to the quote mentioned at the beginning of this book:

"The Barça of Guardiola has done a lot of harm to football"

It is unquestionable that the football proposed by Pep Guardiola has been misinterpreted on many occasions. Too often it has been copied superficially, devaluing and misrepresenting its essence. It is possible that many of the coaches who try to emulate the Pep Team confuse the model of play with the style of play, and that there is also confusion about the importance of ball possession (being a means and not an aim in itself). Maybe, when the games of that brilliant team were broadcast on TV, the following caption should have been shown: "Do not try this at home"!

However, do not be cynical. It is possible. People who cannot do it themselves will say you cannot do it. You may accomplish excellence in the model of play if you understand its complexity and master its detail. I hope this book provides the reader with the framework, tools and inspiration to believe that the beautiful game can be played by a dreamer, when shown that *it can be done*. A way no one could think of before, and which no one will ever forget.

Bennion Kearny publishes a lot of books
for the Soccer Coach.

You can see all our soccer books at:

www.BennionKearny.com/Soccer

<< Or click on the QR code to the right >>

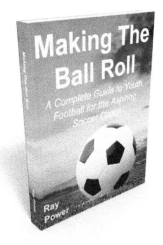

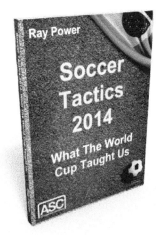

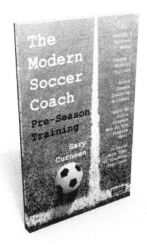

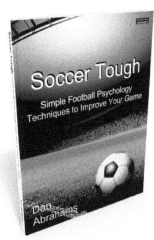

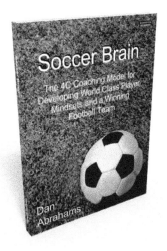

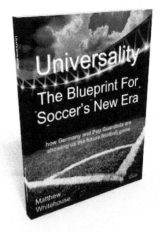

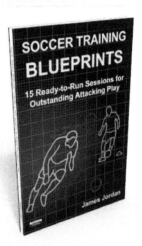

Plus Many More...

www.BennionKearny.com/Soccer

Lightning Source UK Ltd.
Milton Keynes UK
UKHW050951041119
352864UK00009B/1021/P